GLORY TO GOD

HYMNS AND SONGS
FOR ADVENT AND CHRISTMAS

Other products available in the *Glory to God* series

978-0-664-50304-8 (Pew, Presbyterian seal, red)
978-0-664-50313-0 (Pew, Presbyterian seal, purple)
978-0-664-23896-4 (Pew, Ecumenical edition, red)
978-0-664-23897-1 (Pew, Ecumenical edition, purple)
978-0-664-50312-3 (Hymnal companion)
978-0-664-50314-7 (Accompaniment edition, red)
978-0-664-50321-5 (Accompaniment edition, purple)
978-0-664-50342-0 (Accompaniment edition, loose leaf)
978-0-664-50323-9 (Enlarged print, loose leaf)
978-0-664-50322-2 (Enlarged print, text edition, bound)
978-0-664-50324-6 (Gift edition)

GLORY to GOD

HYMNS AND SONGS
FOR ADVENT AND CHRISTMAS

© 2017 Westminster John Knox Press

First edition
Published by Westminster John Knox Press
Louisville, Kentucky

17 18 19 20 21 22 23 24 25 26—10 9 8 7 6 5 4 3 2 1

All rights reserved. No part of this book may be reproduced or transmitted in any form or by any means, electronic or mechanical, including photocopying, recording, or by any information storage or retrieval system, without permission in writing from the publisher. Permission to reprint copyrighted liturgical material, song texts, or music must be obtained from the copyright owners. A complete list of copyright holders may be found in the Acknowledgments, pp. 79–81, and their contact information may be found online at www.pcusastore.com/hymnal. All other requests for permission to reprint must be made in writing to Westminster John Knox Press, 100 Witherspoon Street, Louisville, Kentucky 40202-1396. Or contact us at www.wjkbooks.com.

Every effort has been made to trace the owner or holder of each copyright. If any rights have been inadvertently infringed upon, the publisher asks that the omission be excused and agrees to make the necessary corrections in future printings.

♾ The paper used in this publication meets the minimum requirements of the American National Standard for Information Sciences—Permanence of Paper for Printed Library Materials, ANSI Z39.48-1992.

CONTENTS

Hymns have been renumbered for use in this special Christmas and Advent edition of *Glory to God*. The original hymn numbers from *Glory to God* are in parentheses below. On the hymns themselves, the number for the Advent/Christmas supplement appears above the original hymn number.

Come, Thou Long-Expected Jesus . . . . No. 1 (82)
Come, Thou Long-Expected Jesus . . . . No. 2 (83)
Creator of the Stars of Night . . . . No. 3 (84)
Light One Candle to Watch for Messiah . . . . No. 4 (85)
The People Who Walked in Darkness . . . . No. 5 (86)
Comfort, Comfort Now My People . . . . No. 6 (87)
O Come, O Come, Emmanuel . . . . .No. 7 (88)
For You, O Lord, My Soul in Stillness Waits
   (My Soul in Stillness Waits) . . . . No. 8 (89)
Wait for the Lord (Psalm 27) . . . . .No. 9 (90)
Come, Come Emmanuel . . . . No. 10 (91)
While We Are Waiting, Come . . . . No. 11 (92)
Lift Up Your Heads, Ye Mighty Gates .No. 12 (93)
Now the Heavens Start to Whisper . . . . No. 13 (94)
Prepare the Way of the Lord . . . . .No. 14 (95)
On Jordan's Bank the Baptist's Cry . . . . No. 15 (96)
Watchman, Tell Us of the Night . . . . .No. 16 (97)
To a Maid Whose Name Was Mary . . . . .No. 17 (98)
My Soul Gives Glory to My God (Song of Mary) . . . . No. 18 (99)
My Soul Cries Out with a Joyful Shout
   (Canticle of the Turning) . . . . No. 19 (100)
No Wind at the Window . . . . No. 20 (101)
Savior of the Nations, Come . . . . No. 21 (102)
Come Now, O Prince of Peace (오소서) . . . . No. 22 (103)
O Lord, How Shall I Meet You . . . . No. 23 (104)
People, Look East . . . . No. 24 (105)
Prepare the Way, O Zion . . . . No. 25 (106)
Awake! Awake, and Greet the New Morn . . . . No. 26 (107)
Of the Father's Love Begotten . . . . No. 27 (108)
Blest Be the God of Israel (Song of Zechariah) . . . . No. 28 (109)
Love Has Come . . . . No. 29 (110)
From Heaven Above . . . . No. 30 (111)
On Christmas Night All Christians Sing . . . . No. 31 (112)
Angels We Have Heard on High . . . . No. 32 (113)
Away in a Manger . . . . No. 33 (114)

Away in a Manger	No. 34 (115)
The Snow Lay on the Ground	No. 35 (116)
While Shepherds Watched Their Flocks	No. 36 (117)
While Shepherds Watched Their Flocks	No. 37 (118)
Hark! The Herald Angels Sing	No. 38 (119)
Where Shepherds Lately Knelt	No. 39 (120)
O Little Town of Bethlehem	No. 40 (121)
Silent Night, Holy Night	No. 41 (122)
It Came Upon the Midnight Clear	No. 42 (123)
Still, Still, Still	No. 43 (124)
Before the Marvel of This Night	No. 44 (125)
Jesus, Jesus, Oh, What a Wonderful Child	No. 45 (126)
Hark! The Herald Angels Sing (Jesus, the Light of the World)	No. 46 (127)
Infant Holy, Infant Lowly	No. 47 (128)
Lo, How a Rose E'er Blooming	No. 48 (129)
Break Forth, O Beauteous Heavenly Light	No. 49 (130)
In the Heavens Shone a Star	No. 50 (131)
Good Christian Friends, Rejoice	No. 51 (132)
O Come, All Ye Faithful	No. 52 (133)
Joy to the World	No. 53 (134)
There's a Star in the East (Rise Up, Shepherd, and Follow)	No. 54 (135)
Go, Tell It on the Mountain	No. 55 (136)
He Came Down	No. 56 (137)
Who Would Think That What Was Needed	No. 57 (138)
That Boy-Child of Mary	No. 58 (139)
Once in Royal David's City	No. 59 (140)
On This Day Earth Shall Ring	No. 60 (141)
'Twas in the Moon of Wintertime	No. 61 (142)
Angels, from the Realms of Glory	No. 62 (143)
In the Bleak Midwinter	No. 63 (144)
What Child Is This	No. 64 (145)
Gentle Mary Laid Her Child	No. 65 (146)
The First Nowell	No. 66 (147)
Mary and Joseph Came to the Temple	No. 67 (148)
All Hail to God's Anointed (Psalm 72)	No. 68 (149)
As with Gladness Men of Old	No. 69 (150)
We Three Kings of Orient Are	No. 70 (151)
What Star Is This, with Beams So Bright	No. 71 (152)
In Bethlehem a Newborn Boy	No. 72 (153)
Jesus Entered Egypt	No. 73 (154)
Raise a Song of Gladness	No. 74 (155)
Sing of God Made Manifest	No. 75 (156)
Acknowledgments	79

Come, Thou Long-Expected Jesus 82

1 Come, thou long-expected Jesus, born to set thy people free;
2 Born thy people to deliver, born a child and yet a king,

from our fears and sins release us; let us find our rest in thee.
born to reign in us forever, now thy gracious kingdom bring.

Israel's strength and consolation, hope of all the earth thou art;
By thine own eternal Spirit rule in all our hearts alone;

dear desire of every nation, joy of every longing heart.
by thine all-sufficient merit raise us to thy glorious throne.

With its opening "Come," this hymn sounds the note of entreaty and invitation that characterizes the Advent season (from the Latin *adventus* = "coming"). Its blending of memory and hope helps us to give voice to our present faith as we stand between the past and the future.

TEXT: Charles Wesley, 1744
MUSIC: Rowland Hugh Prichard, 1830; harm. Ralph Vaughan Williams, 1906

HYFRYDOL
8.7.8.7.D
(alternate tune: STUTTGART, 83)

2
83 Come, Thou Long-Expected Jesus

1 Come, thou long-ex-pect-ed Je-sus, born to set thy peo-ple free;
2 Is-rael's strength and con-so-la-tion, hope of all the earth thou art;
3 Born thy peo-ple to de-liv-er, born a child and yet a king,
4 By thine own e-ter-nal Spir-it rule in all our hearts a-lone;

from our fears and sins re-lease us; let us find our rest in thee.
dear de-sire of ev-ery na-tion, joy of ev-ery long-ing heart.
born to reign in us for-ev-er, now thy gra-cious king-dom bring.
by thine all-suf-fi-cient mer-it raise us to thy glo-rious throne.

With its opening "Come," this hymn sounds the note of entreaty and invitation that characterizes the Advent season (from the Latin *adventus* = "coming"). Its blending of memory and hope helps us to give voice to our present faith as we stand between the past and the future.

TEXT: Charles Wesley, 1744
MUSIC: Witt's *Psalmodia Sacra*, 1715, alt.

STUTTGART
8.7.8.7
(alternate tune: HYFRYDOL, 82)

3
84 Creator of the Stars of Night

1 Cre-a-tor of the stars of night, your peo-ple's ev-er-
2 When this old world drew on toward night, you came; but not in
3 At your great name, O Je-sus, now all knees must bend, all
4 To God the Fa-ther, God the Son, and God the Spir-it,

The Latin original of this text for Advent dates from at least the 9th century, and the English version was created a millennium later as part of the 19th-century recovery of early Christian hymns. It is provided here with its traditional plainchant setting.

TEXT: Latin hymn, 9th cent.; trans. John Mason Neale, 1851; as in *The Hymnal* 1940, alt.
MUSIC: Sarum plainsong, Mode IV, 9th cent.; harm. Alfred V. Fedak, 2011
Text Alt. © 1940 Church Pension Fund
Music Harm. © 2011 Alfred V. Fedak

CONDITOR ALME SIDERUM
LM
(alternate harmonization, 671)
(alternate tune: PUER NOBIS NASCITUR)

last - ing light, O Christ, re - deem - er of us all,
splen - dor bright, not as a mon - arch, but the child
hearts must bow: all things on earth with one ac - cord,
Three in One, praise, hon - or, might, and glo - ry be

we pray you, hear us when we call.
of Mar - y, blame - less moth - er mild.
like those in heaven, shall call you Lord.
from age to age e - ter - nal - ly. A - men.

4 Light One Candle to Watch for Messiah

85

1 Light one can - dle to watch for Mes - si - ah: let the
2 Light two can - dles to watch for Mes - si - ah: let the
3 Light three can - dles to watch for Mes - si - ah: let the
4 Light four can - dles to watch for Mes - si - ah: let the

light ban - ish dark - ness. He shall bring sal -
light ban - ish dark - ness. He shall feed the
light ban - ish dark - ness. Lift your heads and
light ban - ish dark - ness. He is com - ing;

va - tion to Is - rael, God ful - fills the prom - ise.
flock like a shep - herd, gent - ly lead them home - ward.
lift high the gate - way for the King of glo - ry.
tell the glad ti - dings. Let your lights be shin - ing.

This text works best when used incrementally during the four weeks of Advent. It underscores the "waiting" theme of the season and concludes appropriately with reference to Matthew 25:1–13. The tune name meaning "deep in the forest" comes from the opening of a Yiddish love song.

TEXT: Wayne L. Wold, 1984
MUSIC: Yiddish folk song; arr. Wayne L. Wold, 1984
Text and Music Arr. © 1984 Fortress Press (admin. Augsburg Fortress)

TIF IN VELDELE
10.7.9.6

Comfort, Comfort Now My People

6
87

1 "Com-fort, com-fort now my peo-ple; tell of peace!" So says our God.
2 For the her-ald's voice is cry-ing in the des-ert far and near,
3 Straight shall be what long was crook-ed, and the rough-er plac-es plain.

"Com-fort those who sit in dark-ness mourn-ing un-der sor-row's load.
call-ing us to true re-pen-tance, since the reign of God is here.
Let your hearts be true and hum-ble, as be-fits God's ho-ly reign.

To my peo-ple now pro-claim that my par-don waits for them!
O, that warn-ing cry o-bey! Now pre-pare for God a way.
For the glo-ry of the Lord now on earth is shed a-broad,

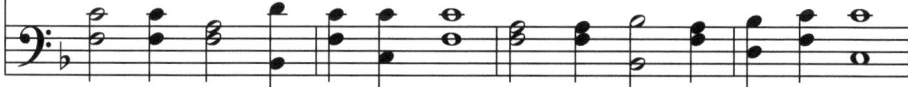

Tell them that their sins I cov-er, and their war-fare now is o-ver."
Let the val-leys rise in meet-ing and the hills bow down in greet-ing.
and all flesh shall see the to-ken that God's word is nev-er bro-ken.

This 17th-century German paraphrase of Isaiah 40:1–5 was one of the texts translated as part of the 19th-century British interest in German religious poetry. It is set here to one of the most popular Genevan Psalter tunes, probably derived from an earlier French folk song.

TEXT: Johannes Olearius, 1671; trans. Catherine Winkworth, 1863, alt.
MUSIC: Genevan Psalter, 1551

GENEVAN 42
8.7.8.7.7.7.8.8

88 O Come, O Come, Emmanuel

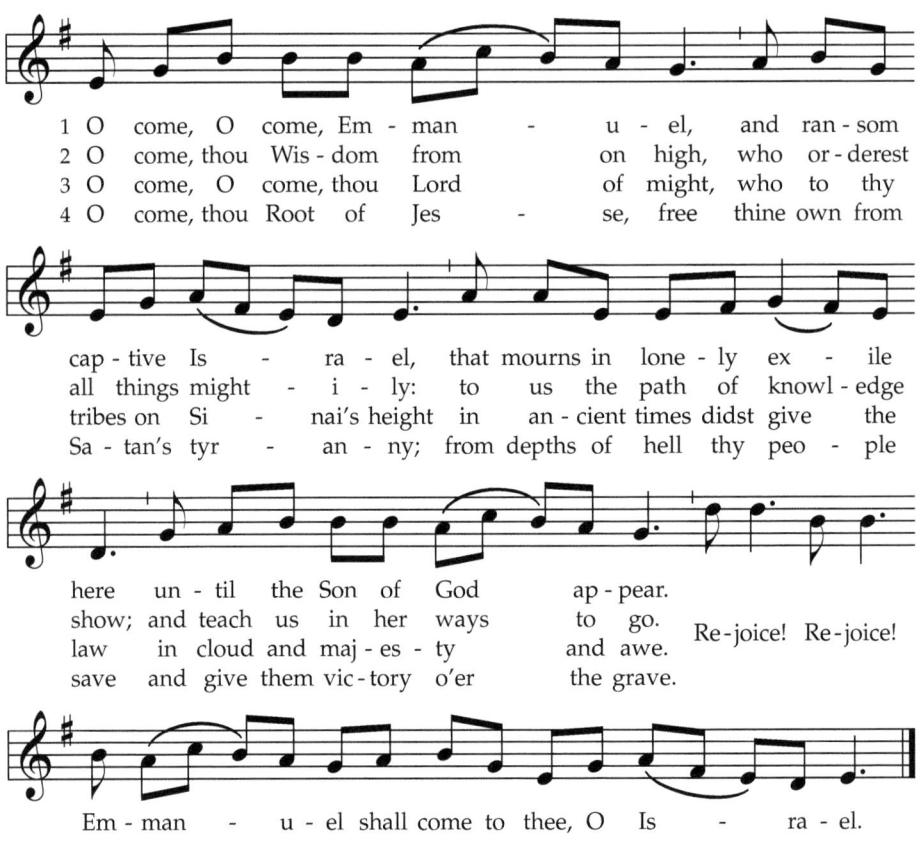

1. O come, O come, Emmanuel, and ransom captive Israel, that mourns in lonely exile here until the Son of God appear.
2. O come, thou Wisdom from on high, who orderest all things mightily: to us the path of knowledge show; and teach us in her ways to go.
3. O come, O come, thou Lord of might, who to thy tribes on Sinai's height in ancient times didst give the law in cloud and majesty and awe. Rejoice! Rejoice!
4. O come, thou Root of Jesse, free thine own from Satan's tyranny; from depths of hell thy people save, and give them victory o'er the grave.

Emmanuel shall come to thee, O Israel.

5. O come, thou Key of David, come,
and open wide our heavenly home;
make safe the way that leads on high,
and close the path to misery.
    Rejoice! Rejoice! Emmanuel
    shall come to thee, O Israel.

6. O come, thou Dayspring, come and cheer
our spirits by thine advent here;
disperse the gloomy clouds of night,
and death's dark shadows put to flight.
    Rejoice! Rejoice! Emmanuel
    shall come to thee, O Israel.

7. O come, Desire of nations, bind
all peoples in one heart and mind;
bid envy, strife, and discord cease;
fill the whole world with heaven's peace.
    Rejoice! Rejoice! Emmanuel
    shall come to thee, O Israel.

One stanza of this paraphrase of the great O Antiphons may be sung on each of the last days of Advent as follows:

Dec. 17: O Wisdom (2)
Dec. 18: O Lord of might (3)
Dec. 19: O Root of Jesse (4)

Dec. 20: O Key of David (5)
Dec. 21: O Dayspring (6)
Dec. 22: O Desire of Nations (7)

Dec. 23: O Emmanuel (1)

These titles of the coming Christ appeared in daily Vesper antiphons sung during the week before Christmas; their roots date at least to the reign of Charlemagne. Both text and tune are the fruit of 19th-century efforts to reclaim Christian treasures from pre-Reformation sources.

TEXT: Latin prose, pre-9th cent.; trans. composite
MUSIC: Plainsong; adapt. Thomas Helmore, 1852; arr. John Weaver, 1988
Music Arr. © 1990 John Weaver

VENI EMMANUEL
LM with refrain

For You, O Lord, My Soul in Stillness Waits
My Soul in Stillness Waits

For you, O Lord, my soul in still-ness waits; tru-ly my hope is in you.

1 O Lord of Light, our on - ly hope of glo - ry,
2 O Spring of Joy, rain down up - on our spir - its;
3 O Root of Life, im - plant your seed with - in us,
4 O Key of Knowl - edge, guide us in our pil - grim-age;
5 Come, let us bow be - fore the God who made us;
6 Here we shall meet the Mak - er of the heav - ens,

your ra-diance shines in all who look to you; come, light the
our thirst - y hearts are yearn - ing for your word; come, make us
and in your ad - vent, draw us all to you, our hope re -
we ev - er seek, yet un - ful-filled re - main; o - pen to
let ev - ery heart be o - pened to the Lord, for we are
Cre - a - tor of the moun-tains and the seas, Lord of the

hearts of all in dark and shad - ow.
whole, be com - fort to our hearts.
born in dy - ing and in ris - ing.
us the path-way of your peace.
all the peo - ple of God's hand.
stars, and pres - ent to us now.

With a paraphrase of Psalm 62:5 as a refrain, this Advent text adapts four of the "Great O" antiphons (all of which can be seen in no. 88), combining them with a paraphrase of Psalm 95:6–7 and an echo of a medieval hymn. This rich blend yields a wealth of imagery and meaning.

TEXT and MUSIC: Marty Haugen, 1982
Text and Music © 1982 GIA Publications, Inc.

MY SOUL IN STILLNESS WAITS
Irregular

9
90
Wait for the Lord
(Psalm 27)

Refrain

Wait for the Lord, whose day is near.

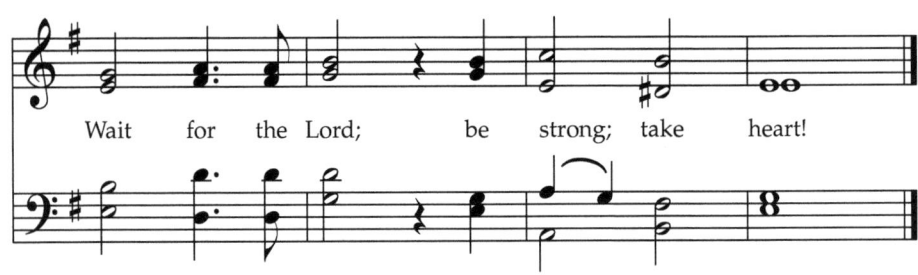

Wait for the Lord; be strong; take heart!

PSALM 27

Refrain

1. The LORD is my light and my salvation;
   whom then shall I fear?
     the LORD is the strength of my life;
     of whom then shall I be afraid?

2. **When evildoers came upon me to eat up my flesh,**
   it was they, my foes and my adversaries, who stumbled and fell.

3. Though an army should encamp against me,
   yet my heart shall not be afraid;
     and though war should rise up against me,
     yet will I put my trust in the LORD.

4. One thing have I asked of the LORD;
   one thing I seek;
     that I may dwell in the house of the LORD all the days of my life;
     to behold the fair beauty of the LORD,
     to seek God in the temple. *Refrain*

5. For on the day of trouble the LORD shall shelter me in safety;
   the LORD shall hide me in the secrecy of the holy place
   and set me high upon a rock.

6. **Even now the LORD lifts up my head**
   above my enemies round about me.
     Therefore I will offer in the holy place an oblation
     with sounds of great gladness;
     I will sing and make music to the LORD. *Refrain*

The refrain for this psalm, drawn from Psalm 27:14, comes from the ecumenical Community of Taizé in France and is most effective when sung in parts. With repeated singing, it can also be used by itself as a contemplative prayer and is especially appropriate in Advent.

TEXT: Ref. Taizé Community, 1984
MUSIC: Jacques Berthier, 1984
Text Ref. and Music © 1984 Les Presses de Taizé (admin. GIA Publications, Inc.)
Responsive Reading © 1993 by Order of Saint Benedict (Published by Liturgical Press)

WAIT FOR THE LORD
8.8

7 Hearken to my voice, O LORD, when I call;
   have mercy on me and answer me.

8 **You speak in my heart and say, "Seek my face."
   Your face, LORD, will I seek.**

9 Hide not your face from me,
   nor turn away your servant in displeasure.

   **You have been my helper;
   cast me not away;
   do not forsake me, O God of my salvation.**

10 Though my father and my mother forsake me,
   the LORD will sustain me.   *Refrain*

11 Show me your way, O LORD;
   lead me on a level path, because of my enemies.

12 **Deliver me not into the hand of my adversaries,
   for false witnesses have risen up against me,
   and also those who speak malice.**

13 What if I had not believed
   that I should see the goodness of the LORD
   in the land of the living!

14 **O tarry and await the LORD's pleasure;
   be strong, and the LORD shall comfort your heart;
   wait patiently for the LORD.**   *Refrain*

Come, Come Emmanuel

1091

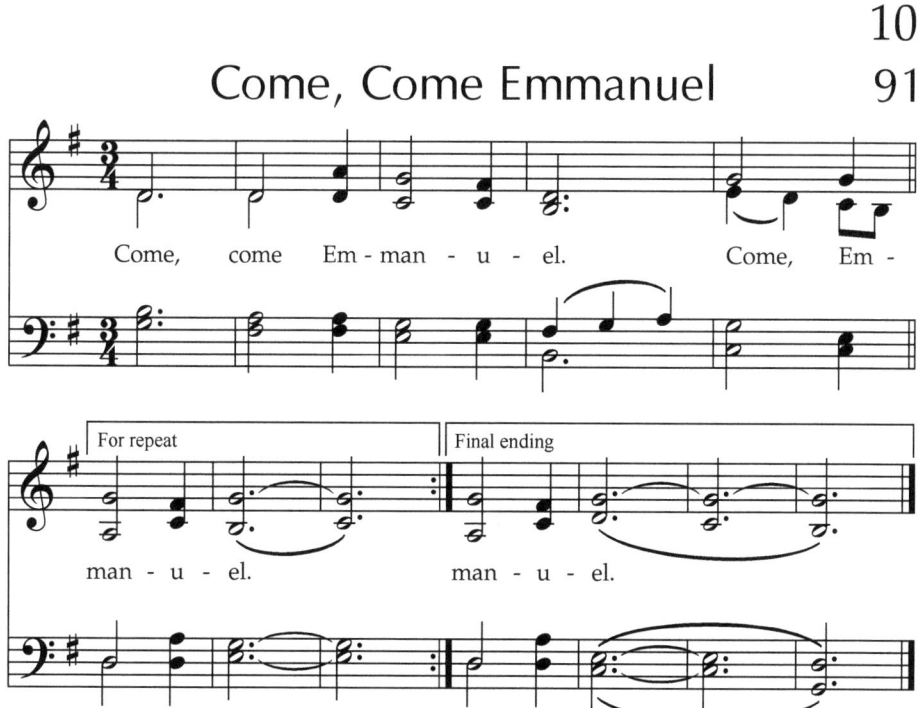

This Advent refrain centers on the name of Jesus meaning "God with us" (Matthew 1:23, quoting Isaiah 7:14). Intended for repeated congregational singing, it can be expanded by the addition of stanzas sung by a soloist or choir, or it can serve effectively as a prayer response.

TEXT and MUSIC: James J. Chepponis, 1995
Text and Music © 1995 GIA Publications, Inc.

11 / 92 While We Are Waiting, Come

1 While we are waiting, come; / while we are waiting, come.
2 With power and glory, come; / with power and glory, come.
3 Come, Savior, quickly come; / come, Savior, quickly come.

Jesus, our Lord, Emmanuel, / while we are waiting, come.

This simple and meditative Advent hymn is so uncomplicated in both text and tune that it can be learned quickly and sung without reference to a book, which might make it effective as a prayer response. It would also lend itself to improvised stanzas on appropriate occasions.

TEXT: Claire Cloninger, 1986
MUSIC: Don Cason, 1986
Text and Music © 1986 Word Music, LLC (admin. WB Music Corp.)

WAITING (Cason)
SM

Lift Up Your Heads, Ye Mighty Gates

12
93

1 Lift up your heads, ye might-y gates; be-hold the King of glo-ry waits; the King of kings is draw-ing near; the Sav-ior of the world is here.
2 Fling wide the por-tals of your heart; make it a tem-ple, set a-part from earth-ly use for heaven's em-ploy, a-dorned with prayer and love and joy.
3 Re-deem-er, come! I o-pen wide my heart to thee; here, Lord, a-bide. Let me thy in-ner pres-ence feel; thy grace and love in me re-veal.

Beginning as a paraphrase of Psalm 24:7–10, this text then applies the door imagery to the singer's heart, and concludes with the individual's welcome of the approaching Savior. It is set to a very effective anonymous 18th-century English tune that has served many texts.

TEXT: Georg Weissel, 1642; trans. Catherine Winkworth, 1855, 1863
MUSIC: *Musica Sacra*, c. 1778

TRURO
LM

This Advent text artfully interweaves what is hidden and what is revealed, primarily in the coming of the long-awaited Messiah. But Christ himself taught us about another hidden truth, his presence in the "least of these" (Matthew 25:40, 45), whom we are also called to welcome.

TEXT: Mary Louise Bringle, 2005
MUSIC: Alexander Johnson's *Tennessee Harmony*, 1818; harm. *Lutheran Book of Worship*, 1978
Text © 2006 GIA Publications, Inc.
Music Harm. © 1978 Lutheran Book of Worship (admin. Augsburg Fortress)

JEFFERSON
8.7.8.7.D

planted, child to spring from Jesse's stem! Like the soil beneath the frost-line, hearts grow soft to welcome him.
splendor, gleams within a world grown dim. Heaven's ember fans to fullness; hearts grow warm to welcome him.
stranger, in the outcast, hid from view: child who comes to grace the manger, teach our hearts to welcome you.

Prepare the Way of the Lord

14 95

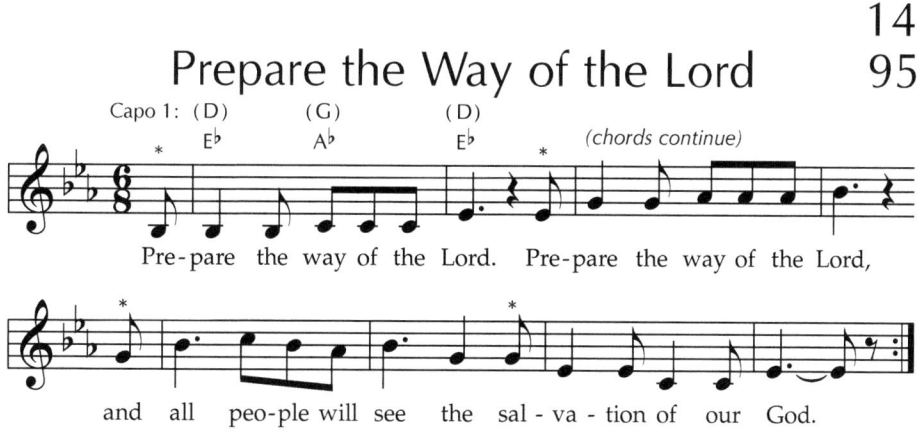

Prepare the way of the Lord. Prepare the way of the Lord, and all people will see the salvation of our God.

*May be sung as a canon.

All three Synoptic Gospels identify John the Baptist as the forerunner of the Messiah (Matthew 3:3/Mark 1:2–3/Luke 3:4) in accord with Isaiah's prophecy (Isaiah 40:3b). Because the latter part of the text (Isaiah 52:10b) has yet to be accomplished, this is still our mission today.

TEXT: Taizé Community, 1984
MUSIC: Jacques Berthier, 1984
Text and Music © 1984 Les Presses de Taizé (admin. GIA Publications, Inc.)

PREPARE THE WAY
7.7.6.7

15
96 On Jordan's Bank the Baptist's Cry

1 On Jordan's bank the Baptist's cry announces that the Lord is nigh; awake and hearken, for he brings glad tidings of the King of kings!
2 Then cleansed be every life from sin; make straight the way for God within, and let us all our hearts prepare for Christ to come and enter there.
3 We hail you as our Savior, Lord, our refuge and our great reward; without your grace we waste away like flowers that wither and decay.
4 Stretch forth your hand; our health restore, and make us rise to fall no more. O let your face upon us shine and fill the world with love divine.

This hymn shows how once-unconnected parts can work together. The text about John the Baptist was written in Latin in the 18th century and translated into English in the 19th century. Similarly, the 17th-century melody was adapted to its present form in the 19th century.

TEXT: Charles Coffin, 1736; trans. John Chandler, 1837, alt.
MUSIC: *Musikalisches Handbuch,* 1690; harm. William Henry Monk, 1847, alt.

WINCHESTER NEW
LM
(alternate tune: PUER NOBIS NASCITUR)

17
98 To a Maid Whose Name Was Mary

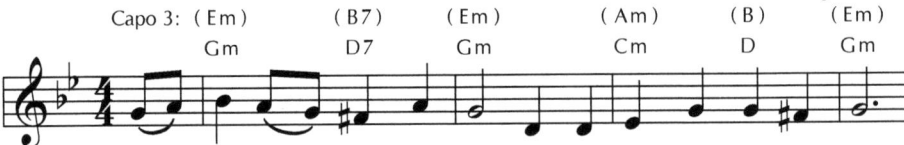

1. To a maid whose name was Mar-y, the an-gel Ga-briel came.
2. "For you are high-ly fa-vored by God the Lord of all,
3. But Mar-y was most trou-bled to hear the an-gel's word.
4. "Fear not, for God is with you, and you shall bear a child.
5. "How shall this be?" said Mar-y, "I am not yet a wife."
6. As Mar-y heard the an-gel, she won-dered at his words.

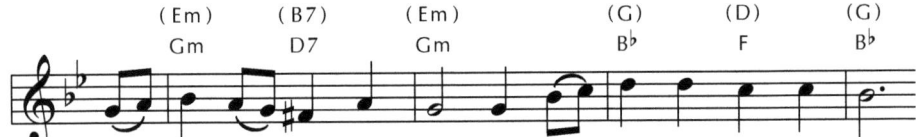

"Fear not," the an-gel told her, "I come to bring good news;
who e-ven now is with you. You are on earth most blest;
What was the an-gel say-ing? It trou-bled her to hear,
His name shall be called Je-sus, God's off-spring from on high.
The an-gel an-swered quick-ly, "The power of the Most High
"Be-hold, I am your hand-maid," she said un-to her God.

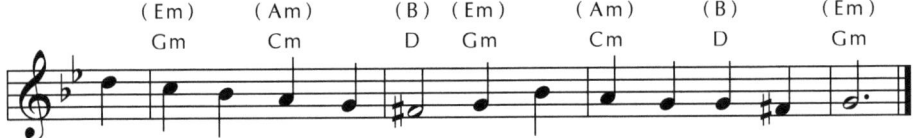

good news I come to tell you, good news, I say, good news."
you are most blest, most bless-ed; God chose you, you are blest!"
to hear the an-gel's mes-sage, it trou-bled her to hear.
And he shall reign for-ev-er, for-ev-er reign on high."
will come up-on you short-ly, your child shall be God's child."
"So be it; I am read-y ac-cord-ing to your word."

Guitar chords do not correspond with keyboard harmony.

This 20th-century ballad-like retelling of the Annunciation (Luke 1:26–38) displays many characteristics of a folk-song style, especially repetition in both text and tune and short quotations included in the narrative. Such features help to make a song both memorable and singable.

TEXT: Gracia Grindal, 1982, alt.
MUSIC: Rusty Edwards, 1982
Text and Music © 1984 Hope Publishing Company

ANNUNCIATION
7.6.7.6.7.6

My Soul Gives Glory to My God
Song of Mary

1. My soul gives glory to my God; my heart pours out its praise. God lifted up my lowliness in many marvelous ways.
2. My God has done great things for me: yes, holy is God's name. All people will declare me blessed, and blessings they shall claim.
3. From age to age to all who fear, such mercy love imparts, dispensing justice far and near, dismissing selfish hearts.
4. Love casts the mighty from their thrones, promotes the insecure, leaves hungry spirits satisfied; the rich seem suddenly poor.
5. Praise God, whose loving covenant supports those in distress, remembering past promises with present faithfulness.

This 20th-century paraphrase is based on the Song of Mary (Luke 1:46–55), commonly known by its opening Latin word, *Magnificat*. This song of praise offers clear reminders that God's purposes often lead to the reversal of human values, exalting the poor and dethroning the mighty.

TEXT: Miriam Therese Winter, 1978; rev. 1987
MUSIC: Wyeth's *Repository of Sacred Music*, 1813; harm. C. Winfred Douglas, 1940
Text © 1978, 1987 Medical Mission Sisters
Music Harm. © 1943, 1961, 1985 Church Pension Fund

MORNING SONG
CM

19
100 My Soul Cries Out with a Joyful Shout
Canticle of the Turning

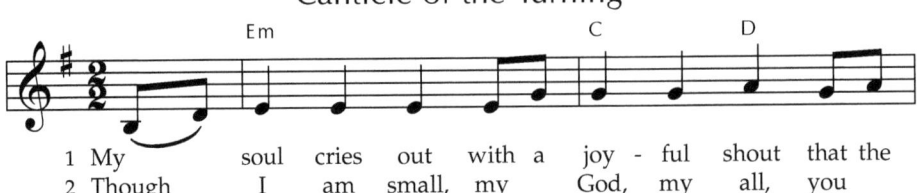

1 My soul cries out with a joy-ful shout that the
2 Though I am small, my God, my all, you
3 From the halls of power to the for-tress tower, not a
4 Though the na-tions rage from age to age, we re-

God of my heart is great, and my spir-it sings of the
work great things in me, and your mer-cy will last from the
stone will be left on stone. Let the king be-ware for your
mem-ber who holds us fast: God's mer-cy must de-

won-drous things that you bring to the ones who wait.
depths of the past to the end of the age to be.
jus-tice tears ev-ery ty-rant from his throne.
liv-er us from the con-quer-or's crush-ing grasp.

You fixed your sight on your ser-vant's plight, and my
Your ver-y name puts the proud to shame, and to
The hun-gry poor shall weep no more, for the
This sav-ing word that our fore-bears heard is the

weak-ness you did not spurn, so from east to west shall my
those who would for you yearn, you will show your might, put the
food they can nev-er earn; there are ta-bles spread; ev-ery
prom-ise which holds us bound, till the spear and rod can be

By employing an energetic Irish folk song for its melody, this ballad-like paraphrase of the Magnificat, Mary's song at her meeting with her relative Elizabeth (Luke 1:46–55), recaptures both the wonder and the faith of the young woman who first recognized what God was doing.

TEXT: Rory Cooney, 1990
MUSIC: Irish melody; arr. Rory Cooney, 1990
Text and Music Arr. © 1990 GIA Publications, Inc.

STAR OF THE COUNTY DOWN
Irregular

Savior of the Nations, Come

21
102

1 Savior of the nations, come; virgin's son, make here your home. Marvel now, O heaven and earth, that the Lord chose such a birth.
2 From God's heart the Savior speeds; back to God his pathway leads; out to vanquish death's command, back to reign at God's right hand.
3 Now your manger, shining bright, hallows night with newborn light. Night cannot this light subdue; let our faith shine ever new.
4 Praise we sing to Christ the Lord, virgin's son, incarnate Word! To the holy Trinity praise we sing eternally.

Though some hymns attributed to Ambrose are doubtful, this one seems rather surely to be by him. Luther's German version (commemorated in the tune name) dropped one syllable from each line of the Latin text, giving the hymn its characteristically declarative Lutheran form.

TEXT: Attr. Ambrose of Milan, 4th cent.; German para. Martin Luther, 1523;
English trans. stanza 1, William Morton Reynolds, 1850, alt.;
English trans. stanzas 2–4, *Evangelical Lutheran Worship*, 2006
MUSIC: Erfurt *Enchiridion*, 1524; harm. Sethus Calvisius, 1594
English Trans. Sts. 2–4 © 2006 Augsburg Fortress

NUN KOMM, DER HEIDEN HEILAND
7.7.7.7

103 Come Now, O Prince of Peace
오소서

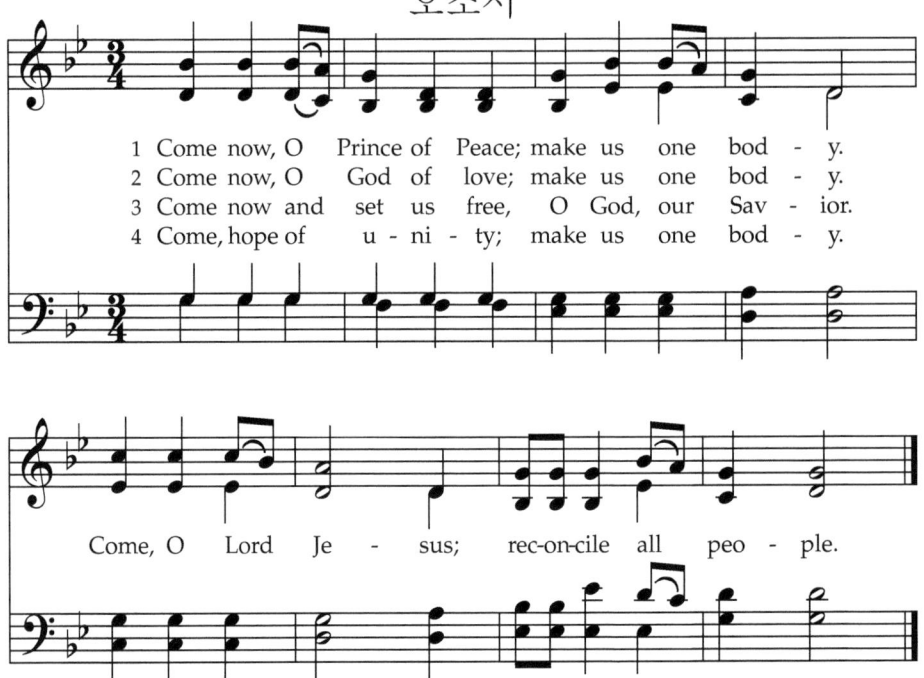

KOREAN

1 오소서 오소서 평화의 임금
우리가 한몸 이루게 하소서

2 오소서 오소서 사랑의 임금
우리가 한몸 이루게 하소서

3 오소서 오소서 자유의 임금
우리가 한몸 이루게 하소서

4 오소서 오소서 통일의 임금
우리가 한몸 이루게 하소서

Originally created for a 1988 world conference for the peace and reunification of the Korean peninsula, these four stanzas centering on peace, love, freedom, and unity demonstrate how texts for particular situations can become hymns that speak deeply to shared human longings.

TEXT: Geonyong Lee, 1988; English trans. Marion Pope, c. 1990
MUSIC: Geonyong Lee, 1988
Text and Music © 1988 Geonyong Lee

O-SO-SO
6.5.5.6

24 / 105 People, Look East

1 People, look east. The time is near of the crowning of the year. Make your house fair as you are able; trim the hearth and set the table.
2 Furrows, be glad. Though earth is bare, one more seed is planted there. Give up your strength the seed to nourish, that in course the flower may flourish.
3 Birds, though you long have ceased to build, guard the nest that must be filled. Even the hour when wings are frozen God for fledging time has chosen.
4 Stars, keep the watch. When night is dim one more light the bowl shall brim, shining beyond the frosty weather, bright as sun and moon together.
5 Angels, announce with shouts of mirth Christ who brings new life to earth. Set every peak and valley humming with the word, the Lord is coming.

This text was written to provide a new Advent text for an existing carol tune, here named for the city in eastern France where it originated. The author has imaginatively expressed the cosmic implications of Christ's coming by addressing each stanza to a part of creation.

TEXT: Eleanor Farjeon, 1928, alt.
MUSIC: French folk melody; harm. Martin Shaw, 1928
Text © 1960 David Higham Associates, Ltd.
Music Harm. © 1928 Oxford University Press

BESANÇON
8.7.9.8.8.7

Prepare the Way, O Zion

1. Prepare the way, O Zion, your Christ is drawing near!
Let every hill and valley a level way appear.
Greet One who comes in glory, foretold in sacred story.

2. He brings God's rule, O Zion; he comes from heaven above.
His rule is peace and freedom, and justice, truth, and love.
Lift high your praise resounding, for grace and joy abounding.

3. Fling wide your gates, O Zion; your Savior's rule embrace,
and tidings of salvation proclaim in every place.
All lands will bow rejoicing, their adoration voicing.

Refrain
O blest is Christ who came in God's most holy name.

Guitar chords do not correspond with keyboard harmony.

This engaging Advent text based on Isaiah 40:3–5 and Psalm 24:7–10 has been in use in the Church of Sweden for almost two hundred years. It is set to a version of an even older Swedish tune, which in turn seems to be derived from a German folktune that spread to Scandinavia.

TEXT: Frans Mikael Franzén, 1812; rev. 1819; trans. Augustus Nelson, 1958; adapt. Charles P. Price, 1980, alt.
MUSIC: *Then Swenska Psalmboken*, 1697; arr. *American Lutheran Hymnal*, 1930
Text © 1982 Hope Publishing Company

BEREDEN VÄG FÖR HERRAN
7.6.7.6.7.7 with refrain

26 / 107 Awake! Awake, and Greet the New Morn

1 A-wake! A-wake, and greet the new morn, for an - gels
2 To us, to all in sor - row and fear, Em - man - u -
3 In dark - est night his com - ing shall be, when all the
4 Re - joice, re - joice, take heart in the night. Though dark the

her - ald its dawn-ing. Sing out your joy, for soon he is
el comes a - sing - ing; his hum - ble song is qui - et and
world is de - spair - ing, as morn - ing light so qui - et and
win - ter and cheer - less, the ris - ing sun shall crown you with

born, be-hold! the Child of our long - ing. Come as a ba - by
near, yet fills the earth with its ring - ing; mu - sic to heal the
free, so warm and gen - tle and car - ing. Then shall the mute break
light; be strong and lov - ing and fear - less. Love be our song and

weak and poor, to bring all hearts to - geth - er, he o - pens
bro - ken soul and hymns of lov - ing - kind - ness. The thun - der
forth in song, the lame shall leap in won - der, the weak be
love our prayer and love our end - less sto - ry; may God fill

wide the heaven - ly door and lives now in - side us for - ev - er.
of his an - thems rolls to shat - ter all ha - tred and vio - lence.
raised a - bove the strong, and weap-ons be bro - ken a - sun - der.
ev - ery day we share and bring us at last in - to glo - ry.

After attending a carol concert, the author and composer of this hymn was moved to create a contemporary, accessible carol that drew on the familiar images in a new way. There are echoes here of passages such as Isaiah 9:6, Isaiah 7:14/Matthew 1:23, Isaiah 35:5–6, Isaiah 2:4.

TEXT: Marty Haugen, 1983, alt.
MUSIC: Marty Haugen, 1983
Text and Music © 1983 GIA Publications, Inc.

REJOICE, REJOICE
9.8.9.8.8.7.8.9

Of the Father's Love Begotten   108

1 Of   the   Fa-ther's love be-got-ten,   ere the worlds be-gan
2 By   his Word was   all   cre-at-ed;   he com-mand-ed; it
3 O,   that birth for-ev-er   bless-ed   when the   Vir-gin, full
4 This   is   he whom seers in   old   time chant-ed   of with one
5 O   ye heights of   heaven, a-dore   him. An-gel hosts, his prais-
6 Christ, to   thee with   God   the   Fa-ther, and, O   Ho-ly Ghost,

to   be,   he   is   Al-pha and   O-me-ga;   he   the
was done: heaven and earth and depths of   o-cean,   u-ni-
of   grace,   by   the   Ho-ly   Ghost con-ceiv-ing,   bore the
ac-cord,   whom   the   voic-es   of   the   proph-ets   prom-ised
es   sing.   Powers, do-min-ions, bow   be-fore   him,   and   ex-
to   thee,   hymn and chant and   high thanks-giv-ing   and   un-

source, the   end-ing   he,   of   the   things that   are,   that
verse   of   three   in   one,   all   that   sees   the moon's soft
Sav-ior   of   our   race,   and   the   babe,   the world's Re-
in   their   faith-ful word.   Now   he   shines,   the   long-ex-
tol   our   God   and King.   Let   no   tongue   on   earth   be
wea-ried   prais-es   be.   Hon-or,   glo-ry,   and   do-

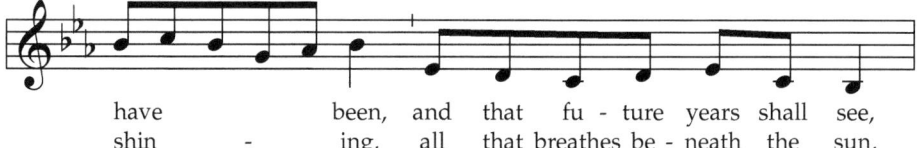

have   been,   and   that   fu-ture   years   shall   see,
shin-ing,   all   that breathes be-neath   the   sun,
deem-er,   first   re-vealed   his   sa-cred   face,
pect-ed.   Let   cre-a-tion   praise   its   Lord,
si-lent;   ev-ery   voice   in   con-cert   ring,
min-ion,   and   e-ter-nal   vic-to-ry,

(after stanza 6)

ev-er-more and ev-er-more!   A-men.

Seldom has the wonder of the Incarnation been expressed so beautifully as in this text, created in the era when the Apostles' and Nicene Creeds were being codified and mindful of similar theological affirmations. It is set here to a plainchant melody from the late Middle Ages.

TEXT: Aurelius Clemens Prudentius, 5th cent.;
trans. John Mason Neale, 1854, alt., and Henry Williams Baker, 1859, alt.
MUSIC: Plainsong, Mode V; harm. C. Winfred Douglas, 1940
Music Harm. © 1943, 1961, 1985 Church Pension Fund

DIVINUM MYSTERIUM
8.7.8.7.8.7.7

28 / 109 Blest Be the God of Israel
Song of Zechariah

1 Blest be the God of Israel, who comes to set us free;
2 God from the house of David a child of grace has given;
3 On those who sit in darkness the sun begins to rise,

who visits and redeems us, who grants us liberty.
a Savior comes among us to raise us up to heaven.
the dawning of forgiveness upon the sinner's eyes.

The prophets spoke of mercy, of freedom and release;
Before him goes the herald, forerunner in the way,
God guides the feet of pilgrims along the paths of peace.

God shall fulfill that promise and bring the people peace.
the prophet of salvation, the harbinger of day.
O bless our God and Savior with songs that never cease!

This 20th-century British paraphrase of the Song of Zechariah (Luke 1:68–79) broadens the implications of what John the Baptist's father says in order to affirm that God's work is ongoing. The tune is named for the composer's oldest sister, who was his first piano teacher.

TEXT: Michael Perry, 1973, alt.
MUSIC: Hal H. Hopson, 1983
Text © 1973 The Jubilate Group (admin. Hope Publishing Company)
Music © 1983 Hope Publishing Company

MERLE'S TUNE
7.6.7.6.D

Love Has Come

29
110

Here is a chance to sing a familiar French carol tune with new words, the most important clearly being "Love." The senses "seen and heard" (as in Acts 4:20 and elsewhere) organize the first two stanzas, while the third holds the summary statement: "Love is the gift of Christmas."

TEXT: Ken Bible, 1996
MUSIC: French melody; arr. Eric T. Myers, 2012
Text © 1996 LNWhymns.com (admin. Music Services)
Music Arr. © 2012 Eric T. Myers

BRING A TORCH
9.9.10.9.9.8

From Heaven Above

30
111

1 "From heaven above to earth I come to bring good news to everyone! Glad tidings of great joy I bring to all the world, and gladly sing:
2 "To you this night is born a child of Mary, chosen virgin mild; this newborn child of lowly birth shall be the joy of all the earth.
3 "This is the Christ, God's Son most high, who hears your sad and bitter cry; he will himself your Savior be and from all sin will set you free."
4 My heart for very joy now leaps; my voice no longer silence keeps; I too must sing with joyful tongue the sweetest ancient cradle-song:
5 "Glory to God in highest heaven, who unto us the Christ has given." With angels sing the Savior's birth, a glad new year to all the earth.

This Christmas hymn gives us a rare glimpse of Martin Luther as a father creating verses for his children to sing at home on Christmas Eve for a retelling of Luke 2:8–14. The first three stanzas paraphrase the angel's song, and the final two provide the human response.

TEXT: Martin Luther, 1535; trans. *Lutheran Book of Worship,* 1978, alt.
MUSIC: Schumann's *Geistliche Lieder,* 1539
Text © 1978 Lutheran Book of Worship **(admin. Augsburg Fortress)**

VOM HIMMEL HOCH
LM

On Christmas Night All Christians Sing

31
112

1. On Christmas night all Christians sing, to hear the news the angels bring; on Christmas night all Christians sing, to hear the news the angels bring, news of great joy, news of great mirth, news of our merciful King's birth.

2. Then why should we on earth be sad, since our Redeemer made us glad; then why should we on earth be sad, since our Redeemer made us glad, when from our sin he set us free, all for to gain our liberty?

3. When sin departs before his grace, then life and health come in its place; when sin departs before his grace, then life and health come in its place; heaven and earth with joy may sing, all for to see the newborn King.

4. All out of darkness we have light, which made the angels sing this night; all out of darkness we have light, which made the angels sing this night: "Glory to God in highest heaven; peace on earth and goodwill. Amen!"

The words of this carol first appeared in 1684 in a collection by an Irish bishop, Luke Wadding. Whether they were his own work or something gleaned from popular use is not clear. The tune name recalls that the tune was collected in 1904 from Mrs. Verrall of Monk's Gate, Sussex.

TEXT: English carol
MUSIC: English carol; arr. Ralph Vaughan Williams, 1912

SUSSEX CAROL
8.8.8.8.8.8

32 / 113 Angels We Have Heard on High

1. Angels we have heard on high, sweetly singing o'er the plains,
and the mountains in reply echoing their joyous strains.
2. Shepherds, why this jubilee? Why your joyous strains prolong?
What the gladsome tidings be which inspire your heavenly song?
3. Come to Bethlehem and see him whose birth the angels sing;
come, adore on bended knee Christ, the Lord, the newborn King.

Refrain
Gloria in excelsis Deo! Gloria in excelsis Deo!

This French carol probably dates from the 1700s, though it was not printed until the following century. Because it uses a vernacular language for the narrative stanzas and Latin for the refrain, it belongs to a special category called "macaronic" or mixed-language texts.

TEXT: French carol; trans. James Chadwick, 1860, alt.
MUSIC: French carol; arr. Edward Shippen Barnes, 1937
Music © 1937, ren. 1965 H. Augustine Smith Jr.
  (admin. Revell Company, a div. of Baker Publishing Group)

GLORIA
7.7.7.7 with refrain

Away in a Manger

33
114

1 A-way in a man-ger, no crib for his bed,
2 The cat-tle are low-ing; the poor ba-by wakes,
3 Be near me, Lord Je-sus; I ask thee to stay

the lit-tle Lord Je-sus laid down his sweet head.
but lit-tle Lord Je-sus, no cry-ing he makes.
close by me for-ev-er and love me, I pray.

The stars in the bright sky looked down where he lay,
I love thee, Lord Je-sus; look down from the sky,
Bless all the dear chil-dren in thy ten-der care,

the lit-tle Lord Je-sus a-sleep on the hay.
and stay by my side un-til morn-ing is nigh.
and fit us for heav-en to live with thee there.

This anonymous carol probably originated among Pennsylvania Lutherans in the late 19th century, giving rise to a mistaken assertion that it had been written by Martin Luther. This tune is also by an American but has become the one usually used in Canada and Great Britain.

TEXT: Stanzas 1–2, *Little Children's Book for Schools and Families,* c. 1885;
stanza 3, Gabriel's *Vineyard Songs,* 1892
MUSIC: William James Kirkpatrick, 1895

CRADLE SONG
11.11.11.11
(alternate tune: MUELLER, 115)

34
115
Away in a Manger

1 A-way in a man-ger, no crib for his bed,
the lit-tle Lord Je-sus laid down his sweet head.
The stars in the bright sky looked down where he lay,
the lit-tle Lord Je-sus a-sleep on the hay.

2 The cat-tle are low-ing; the poor ba-by wakes,
but lit-tle Lord Je-sus, no cry-ing he makes.
I love thee, Lord Je-sus; look down from the sky,
and stay by my side un-til morn-ing is nigh.

3 Be near me, Lord Je-sus; I ask thee to stay
close by me for-ev-er and love me, I pray.
Bless all the dear chil-dren in thy ten-der care,
and fit us for heav-en to live with thee there.

Though erroneously attributed to Martin Luther, this anonymous carol has North American roots, probably originating among Pennsylvania Lutherans. Although more than forty melodies have been connected with these words, this tune was among the earliest written for them.

TEXT: Stanzas 1–2, *Little Children's Book for Schools and Families*, c. 1885;
stanza 3, Gabriel's *Vineyard Songs*, 1892
MUSIC: James R. Murray, 1887

MUELLER
11.11.11.11
(alternate tune: CRADLE SONG, 114)

The Snow Lay on the Ground

35
116

1. The snow lay on the ground; the stars shone bright,
   when Christ our Lord was born on Christ-mas night.
   Ve - ni - te a - do - re - mus Do - mi - num.
   Ve - ni - te a - do - re - mus Do - mi - num.

2. 'Twas gentle Mary maid, so young and strong,
   who welcomed here the Christ-child with a song.
   She laid him in a stall at Beth - le - hem;
   the ass and ox - en shared the roof with them.

3. Saint Joseph too was by to tend the child,
   to guard him, and protect his mother mild.
   The an - gels hov - ered round and sang this song:
   Ve - ni - te a - do - re - mus Do - mi - num.

4. And thus that manger poor became a throne;
   for he whom Mary bore was God the Son.
   O come, then, let us join the heaven - ly host
   to praise the Fa - ther, Son, and Ho - ly Ghost.

Refrain

Ve - ni - te a - do - re - mus Do - mi - num.
Ve - ni - te a - do - re - mus Do - mi - num.

Guitar chords do not correspond with keyboard harmony.

This is one of the few instances where we can see how one Christmas carol has been built upon another. The refrain here quotes the original Latin refrain of "O Come, All Ye Faithful" (see no.52 [133]), which means this text was created later than the first half of the 18th century.

TEXT: Anglo-Irish carol; *Catholic Hymns*, 1860, alt.
MUSIC: Italian folk melody; *Children's Praise*, 1871; harm. Leo Sowerby, 1941
Music Harm. © 1941 Leo Sowerby

VENITE ADOREMUS
10.10.10.10 with refrain

36
117 While Shepherds Watched Their Flocks

1. While shepherds watched their flocks by night, all seated on the ground, the angel of the Lord came down, and glory shone around.
2. "Fear not," said he, for mighty dread had seized their troubled mind: "Glad tidings of great joy I bring to you and humankind.
3. "To you, in David's town this day, is born of David's line the Savior, who is Christ the Lord, and this shall be the sign:
4. "The heavenly babe you there shall find to human view displayed, all humbly wrapped in swathing bands, and in a manger laid."

5. Thus spoke the seraph, and forthwith appeared a shining throng of angels praising God, who thus addressed their joyful song:

6. "All glory be to God on high, and to the earth be peace; good will to all from highest heaven begin and never cease!"

This was one of the first metrical texts to deal with a New Testament narrative rather than paraphrase one of the Psalms. It is set here to a psalm tune that is more than a century older than the words, though the two were not firmly joined until the mid-19th century.

TEXT: Nahum Tate, 1700, alt.
MUSIC: Este's *Psalmes*, 1592; harm. George Kirbye, 1592

WINCHESTER OLD
CM
(alternate tune: CHRISTMAS, 118)

While Shepherds Watched Their Flocks   118

1. While shep-herds watched their flocks by night, all seat-ed
on the ground, the an-gel of the Lord came down, and
glo-ry shone a-round, and glo-ry shone a-round.

2. "Fear not," said he, for might-y dread had seized their
trou-bled mind: "Glad ti-dings of great joy I bring to
you and hu-man-kind, to you and hu-man-kind.

3. "To you, in Da-vid's town this day, is born of
Da-vid's line the Sav-ior, who is Christ the Lord, and
this shall be the sign, and this shall be the sign:

4. "The heaven-ly babe you there shall find to hu-man
view dis-played, all hum-bly wrapped in swath-ing bands, and
in a man-ger laid, and in a man-ger laid."

5. Thus spoke the seraph, and forthwith
appeared a shining throng
of angels praising God, who thus
addressed their joyful song,
addressed their joyful song:

6. "All glory be to God on high,
and to the earth be peace;
good will to all from highest heaven
begin and never cease,
begin and never cease!"

The publication of this text in the late 17th century marked an important moment in the transition from the older practice of psalm-singing to the newer style of hymn-singing. This tune was not originally written for church use but was derived from an operatic aria.

TEXT: Nahum Tate, 1700, alt.
MUSIC: George Frederick Handel, 1728; arr. Lowell Mason, 1821

CHRISTMAS
CM with repeat
(alternate tune: WINCHESTER OLD, 117)

Where Shepherds Lately Knelt   120

1. Where shep-herds late-ly knelt and kept the an-gel's word, I come in half-be-lief, a pil-grim strange-ly stirred. But there is room and wel-come there for me; but there is room and wel-come there for me.

2. In that un-like-ly place I find him as they said: sweet, new-born Babe, how frail, and in a man-ger bed: a still, small voice to cry one day for me; a still, small voice to cry one day for me.

3. How should I not have known I-sa-iah would be there, his proph-e-cies ful-filled? With pound-ing heart, I stare: a child, a son, the Prince of Peace for me; a child, a son, the Prince of Peace for me.

4. Can I, will I for-get how Love was born and burned its way in-to my heart: un-asked, un-forced, un-earned: to die, to live, and not a-lone for me; to die, to live, and not a-lone for me.

Guitar chords do not correspond with keyboard harmony.
  Witnessing the beginning or the end of life evokes very personal responses (emphasized by the "for me" at the end of each stanza), especially when the scale is intimate, as in this imagined visit to Christ's manger. The prophecies recalled in stanza three come from Isaiah 9:6.

TEXT: Jaroslav J. Vajda, 1986
MUSIC: Carl F. Schalk, 1986
Text © 1986 Concordia Publishing House
Music © 1986 GIA Publications, Inc.

MANGER SONG
12.12.10.10

Silent Night, Holy Night!

41
122

1. Silent night, holy night! All is calm, all is bright 'round yon virgin mother and child! Holy Infant, so tender and mild, sleep in heavenly peace, sleep in heavenly peace.

2. Silent night, holy night! Shepherds quake at the sight; glories stream from heaven afar, heavenly hosts sing "Alleluia: Christ the Savior is born; Christ the Savior is born!"

3. Silent night, holy night! Son of God, love's pure light radiant beams from thy holy face, with the dawn of redeeming grace, Jesus, Lord, at thy birth, Jesus, Lord, at thy birth.

4. Silent night, holy night! Wondrous star, lend thy light; with the angels let us sing Alleluia to our King: Christ the Savior is born; Christ the Savior is born.

GERMAN
1. *Stille Nacht, heilige Nacht!*
   Alles schläft, einsam wacht
   nur das traute, hochheilige Paar.
   Holder Knabe im lockigen Haar,
   schlaf in himmlischer Ruh,
   schlaf in himmlischer Ruh!

KOREAN
1. 고요한밤 거룩한밤
   어둠에 묻힌밤
   주의부모 앉아서
   감사기도 드릴때
   아기잘도 잔다
   아기잘도 잔다

SPANISH
1. *¡Noche de paz, noche de amor!*
   Todo duerme en derredor,
   entre los astros que esparcen su luz,
   bella, anunciando al niñito Jesús,
   brilla la estrella de paz,
   brilla la estrella de paz.

The tradition that this carol's tune was created for guitar accompaniment at its first singing on Christmas Eve 1818 seems reliable, though a recent find shows that the text was about two years old. But there is no question that this is now a favorite Christmas carol worldwide.

TEXT: Joseph Mohr, 1816; stanzas 1–3, English trans. John Freeman Young, 1863; stanza 4, English trans. Jane Montgomery Campbell, 1863, alt.
MUSIC: Franz Xaver Gruber, 1818
Korean Trans. © The Christian Literature Society of Korea

STILLE NACHT
Irregular

123 It Came Upon the Midnight Clear

1. It came upon the midnight clear, that glorious song of old,
2. Still through the cloven skies they come, with peaceful wings unfurled,
3. Yet with the woes of sin and strife the world has suffered long;
4. And you, beneath life's crushing load, whose forms are bending low,
5. For lo, the days are hastening on, by prophets seen of old,

from angels bending near the earth, to touch their harps of gold:
and still their heavenly music floats o'er all the weary world:
beneath the heavenly hymn have rolled two thousand years of wrong;
who toil along the climbing way with painful steps and slow,
when with the ever-circling years shall come the time foretold,

"Peace on the earth, good will to all, from heaven's all-gracious King":
above its sad and lowly plains they bend on hovering wing,
and we at war on earth hear not the tidings that they bring;
look now, for glad and golden hours come swiftly on the wing:
when peace shall over all the earth its ancient splendors fling,

The "it" of the first line of this text by a Unitarian minister does not refer to the birth of Jesus, but to "that glorious song of old," the angelic tidings of peace on earth. The restored third stanza laments how often the noise of human strife has obscured that message.

TEXT: Edmund Hamilton Sears, 1849, alt.
MUSIC: Richard Storrs Willis, 1850

CAROL
CMD
(alternate tune: NOEL)

Jesus, Jesus, O What a Wonderful Child 45 126

Specific sources for the words and the music of this piece from the African American heritage remain uncertain. The predictable rhymes suggest that, like "Jesus, the Light of the World" (see no. 46 [127]), it may have originated as a reflection on an existing Christmas carol.

TEXT: African American; alt.
MUSIC: African American; harm. Jeffrey Radford; arr. Horace Clarence Boyer, 2000
Music Harm. © 1992 The Pilgrim Press
Music Arr. © 2000 Horace Clarence Boyer

WONDERFUL CHILD
Irregular

46
127

Hark! The Herald Angels Sing
Jesus, the Light of the World

With a gospel feel

1. Hark! the herald angels sing. Jesus, the light of the world.
2. Joyful all you nations, rise. Jesus, the light of the world.
3. Christ by highest heaven adored; Jesus, the light of the world.
4. Hail, the heaven-born Prince of Peace! Jesus, the light of the world.

Glory to the newborn King, Jesus, the light of the world.
Join the triumph of the skies. Jesus, the light of the world.
Christ, the everlasting Lord; Jesus, the light of the world.
Hail, the Sun of righteousness! Jesus, the light of the world.

This blues-tinged setting of a familiar Christmas carol participates in a longstanding African American practice of adapting Anglo-European texts, as is done here by incorporating a repeated internal line and by appending a refrain that expands that line's language and imagery.

TEXT: Stanzas, Charles Wesley, 1739; ref., George D. Elderkin, 1890
MUSIC: George D. Elderkin, 1890; arr. Evelyn Simpson-Curenton, 2000
Music Arr. © 2000 GIA Publications, Inc.

WE'LL WALK IN THE LIGHT
7.7.7.7 with refrain

130 Break Forth, O Beauteous Heavenly Light

Break forth, O beauteous heavenly light, and usher in the morning. You shepherds, shudder not with fright, but hear the angel's warning. This child, now weak in infancy, our confidence and joy shall be, the power of Satan breaking, our peace eternal making.

This exuberant text, based on Isaiah 9:2–7, was the ninth of twelve stanzas in its original German hymn. The chorale tune associated with this hymn went through many changes at the hands of later composers, reaching its present form in J. S. Bach's *Christmas Oratorio*.

TEXT: Johann Rist, 1641; trans. John Troutbeck, 1873
MUSIC: Johann Schop, 1641; harm. Johann Sebastian Bach, 1734

ERMUNTRE DICH
8.7.8.7.8.8.7.7

50 In the Heavens Shone a Star 131

The collaboration of a Philippine linguist and an American missionary, this text includes the usual harmonized Christmas and Epiphany elements, but they gain a distinctive flavor from the musical setting using the five-note scale of the Kalinga people who live in northern Luzon.

TEXT: Jonathan Malicsi and Ellsworth Chandlee, 20th cent.
MUSIC: Kalinga melody; arr. Joel Navarro, 2010
Text © 1990, 2000 Christian Conference of Asia (admin. GIA Publications, Inc.)
Music © 2010 Faith Alive Christian Resources

KALINGA
7.7.7.7 with refrain

Like other material from oral traditions, 19th-century African American spirituals flourished without being written down. Their refrains were their most stable parts, and narrative stanzas were often improvised to fit. These Nativity stanzas attempt to recall that tradition.

TEXT: African American spiritual; stanzas, John W. Work II, 1940
MUSIC: African American spiritual; arr. John W. Work III, 1940; harm. Melva Wilson Costen, 1987
Music Harm. © 1989 Melva Wilson Costen

GO TELL IT
7.6.7.6 with refrain

He Came Down

56
137

He came down that we may have love; he came down that we may have love; he came down that we may have love; hal-le-lu-jah for-ev-er-more.

Leader: Why did he come?

Additional stanzas:

… that we may have light

… that we may have peace

… that we may have joy

Because this traditional Cameroon piece begins with the refrain, it does not initially reveal that it is cast as a call-and-response song. Assigning the answers to the congregation rather than to the leader is a notable affirmation of the corporate wisdom of God's people.

TEXT: Cameroon song
MUSIC: Cameroon melody; transcr. and arr. John L. Bell, 1986
Music Arr. © 1986 WGRG, Iona Community (admin. GIA Publications, Inc.)

HE CAME DOWN
LM

138 Who Would Think That What Was Needed

1 Who would think that what was needed to transform and save the earth might not be a plan or army, proud in purpose, proved in worth? Who would think, despite derision, that a

2 Shepherds watch and wise men wonder; monarchs scorn and angels sing; such a place as none would reckon hosts a holy helpless thing. Stable beasts and bypassed strangers watch a

3 Centuries of skill and science span the past from which we move, yet experience questions whether, with such progress, we improve. While the human lot we ponder, lest our

Hindsight is nearly always clearer than foresight, and with gentle good humor this Christmas hymn points out how great was the gap between human expectation and God's actual way of providing a means of salvation for us. God's ways continually exceed our claims to comprehend them.

TEXT: John L. Bell and Graham Maule, 1987
MUSIC: John L. Bell, 2005
Text and Music © 1987, 2005 WGRG, Iona Community (admin. GIA Publications, Inc.)

WHITE ROSETTES
8.7.8.7.D

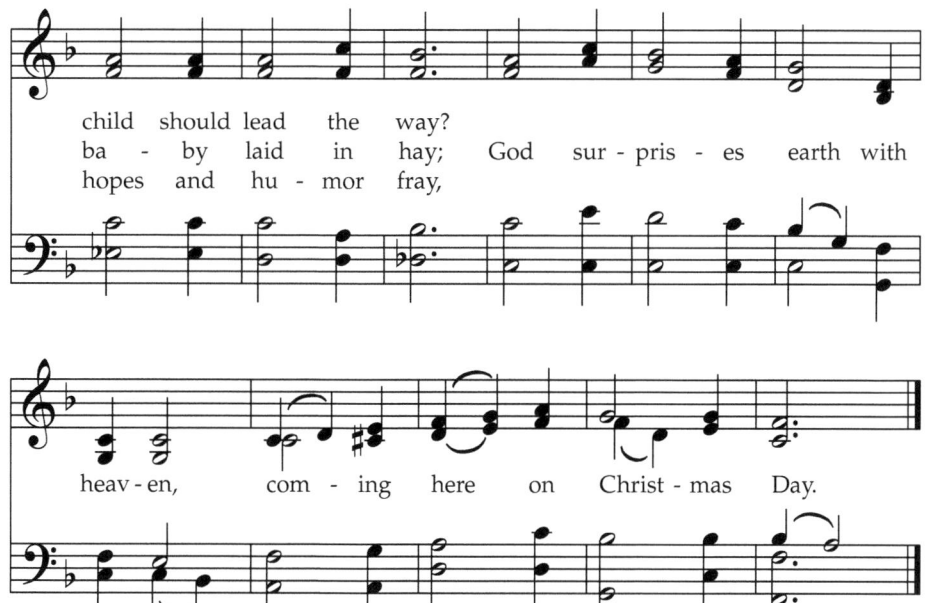

58 / 139 That Boy-Child of Mary

Refrain

That boy-child of Mary was born in a stable, a manger his cradle in Bethlehem.

1. What shall we call him, child of the manger? What name is given in Bethlehem?
2. His name is Jesus, God ever with us, God given for us in Bethlehem.
3. How can he save us; how can he help us, born here among us in Bethlehem?
4. Gift of the Father, to human mother, makes him our brother of Bethlehem.
5. One with the Father, he is our Savior, heaven-sent helper of Bethlehem.
6. Gladly we praise him, love and adore him, give ourselves to him of Bethlehem.

Written by a Scottish missionary for use at St. Michael's Cathedral in Blantyre, Malawi, this hymn on the meaning of Christ's birth and name reflects an aspect of that African culture, where naming often expresses the conditions of a child's birth or hopes for his or her life.

TEXT: Tom Colvin, 1967
MUSIC: Malawi melody; adapt. Tom Colvin, 1967
Text and Music © 1969 Hope Publishing Company

BLANTYRE
Irregular

60 / 141 On This Day Earth Shall Ring

1. On this day earth shall ring with the song
2. His the doom, ours the mirth; when he came
3. God's bright star, o'er his head, wise men three
4. On this day an-gels sing; with their song

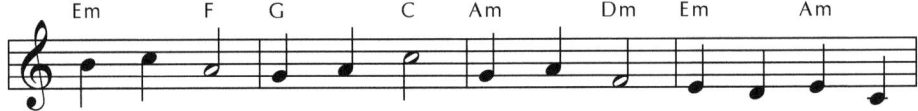

chil-dren sing to the Lord, Christ our King, born on earth to
down to earth Beth-le-hem saw his birth; ox and ass be-
to him led; kneel they low by his bed, lay their gifts be-
earth shall ring, prais-ing Christ, heav-en's King, born on earth to

Refrain

save us; him the Fa-ther gave us.
side him from the cold would hide him.   *Id-e-o - o - o,
fore him, praise him and a-dore him.
save us; peace and love he gave us.

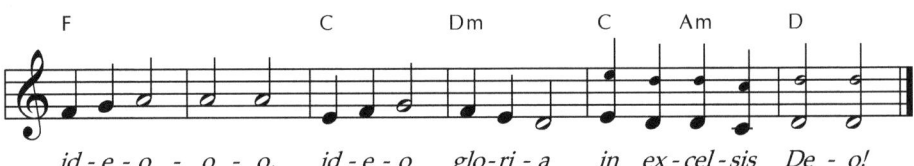

id-e-o - o - o, id-e-o glo-ri-a in ex-cel-sis De-o!

Therefore, glory to God in the highest.

Guitar chords do not correspond with keyboard harmony.

Although this Latin carol for Christmas may have roots several centuries older than its 16th-century emergence, the text was all in one language until its 20th-century translator chose to adopt the original last two lines of the fourth stanza as a unifying refrain in all stanzas.

TEXT: *Piae Cantiones,* 1582; trans. Jane Marian Joseph, c. 1917
MUSIC: *Piae Cantiones,* 1582; arr. Gustav Holst, c. 1917
Text and Music Arr. © 1924, ren. J. Curwen & Sons Ltd.

PERSONENT HODIE
6.6.6.6.6 with refrain

'Twas in the Moon of Wintertime

61
142

1. 'Twas in the moon of win-ter-time, when all the birds had fled,
Great Spir-it, Lord of all the earth sent an-gel choirs in-stead.
Be-fore their light the stars grew dim and wan-dering
hunt-ers heard the hymn:

2. With-in a lodge of bro-ken bark the ten-der babe was found.
A rag-ged robe of rab-bit skin en-wrapped his beau-ty round.
But as the hunt-ers brave drew nigh the an-gel
song rang loud and high:

3. The ear-liest moon of win-ter-time is not so round and fair
as was the ring of glo-ry on the help-less in-fant there.
The chiefs from far be-fore him knelt with gifts of
fox and bea-ver pelt.

4. O chil-dren of the for-est free, the an-gel song is true:
the ho-ly child of earth and heaven is born to-day for you.
Come kneel be-fore the ra-diant boy who brings you
beau-ty, peace, and joy.

Refrain
Je-sus, your king, is born; Je-sus is born. In ex-cel-sis glo-ri-a.

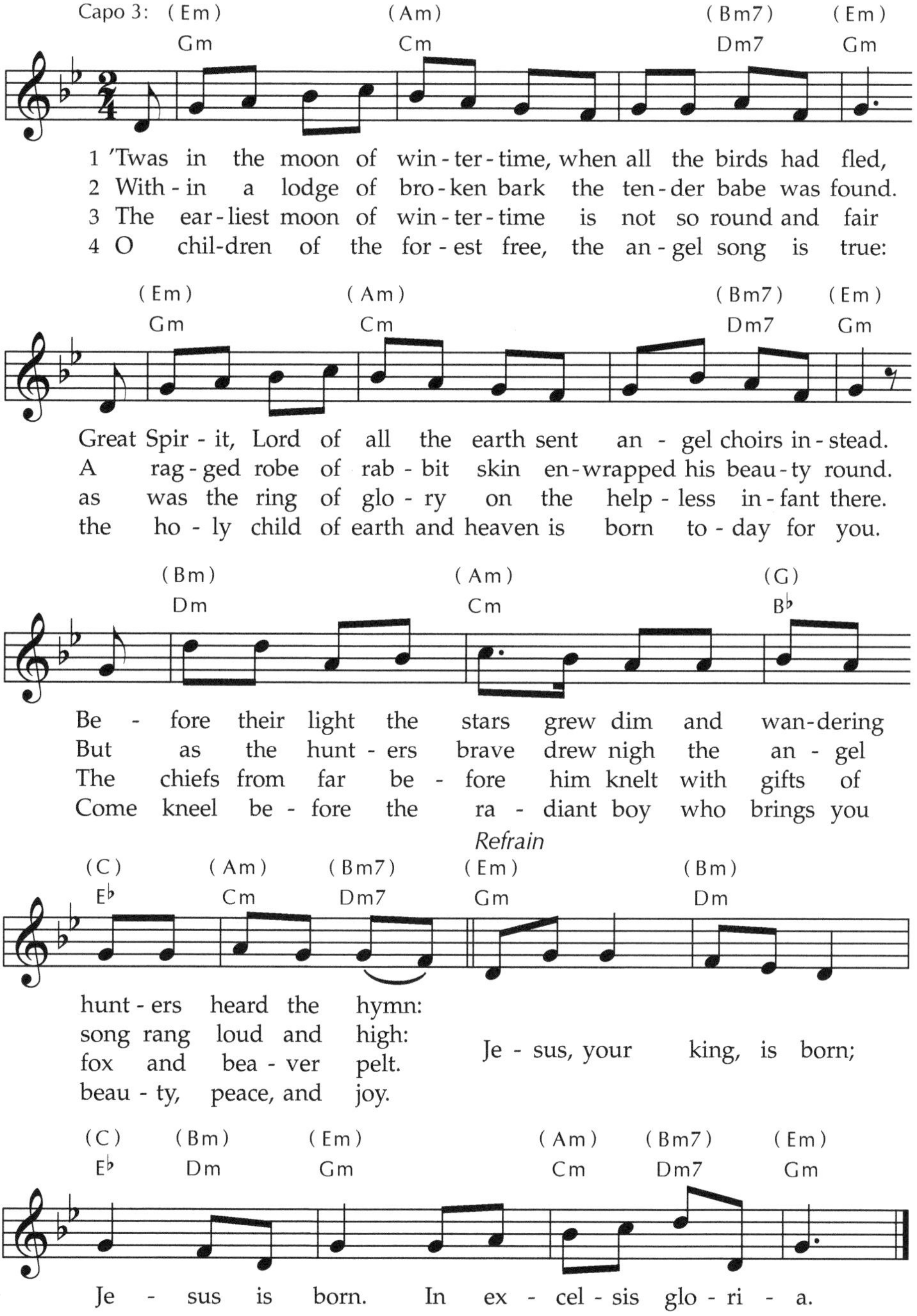

Guitar chords do not correspond with keyboard harmony.

This English text preserves the earliest known Canadian hymn, originally written in the Huron language by a missionary, later translated into French, and eventually paraphrased in English. It is set to a French noël tune old enough to have been used for the original version.

TEXT: Jean de Brébeuf, c. 1641; trans. Jesse Edgar Middleton, 1926, alt.
MUSIC: French folk melody; arr. H. Barrie Cabena, 1970
Music Arr. © 1971 H. Barrie Cabena

UNE JEUNE PUCELLE
8.6.8.6.8.8 with refrain

In the Bleak Midwinter

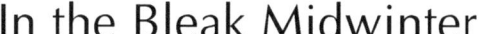

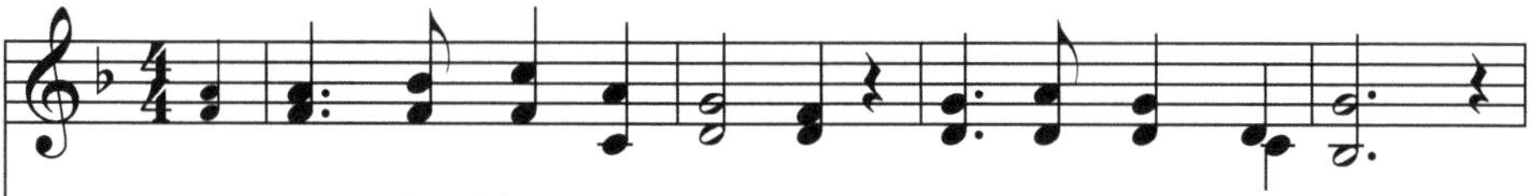

1 In the bleak mid - win - ter, frost - y wind made moan;
2 Our God, heaven can - not hold him, nor earth sus - tain;
3 An - gels and arch - an - gels may have gath - ered there;
4 What can I give him, poor as I am?

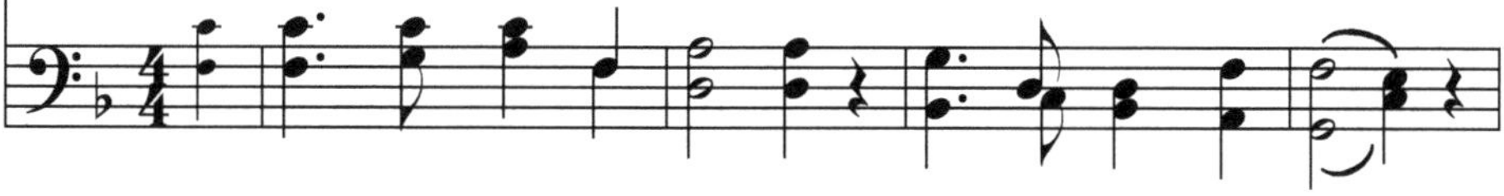

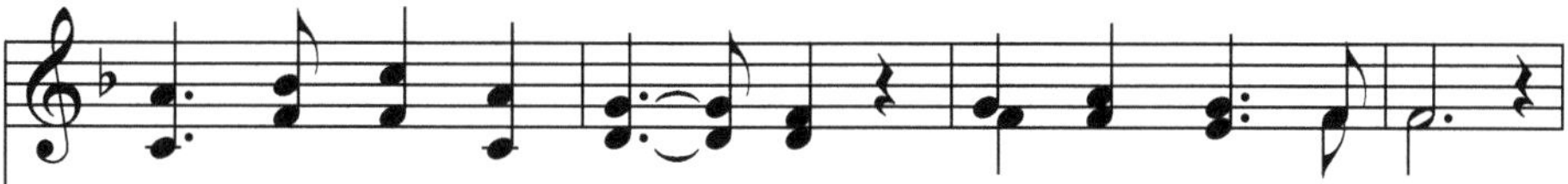

earth stood hard as i - ron, wa - ter like a stone;
heaven and earth shall flee a - way when he comes to reign:
cher - u - bim and ser - a - phim thronged the air;
If I were a shep - herd, I would bring a lamb;

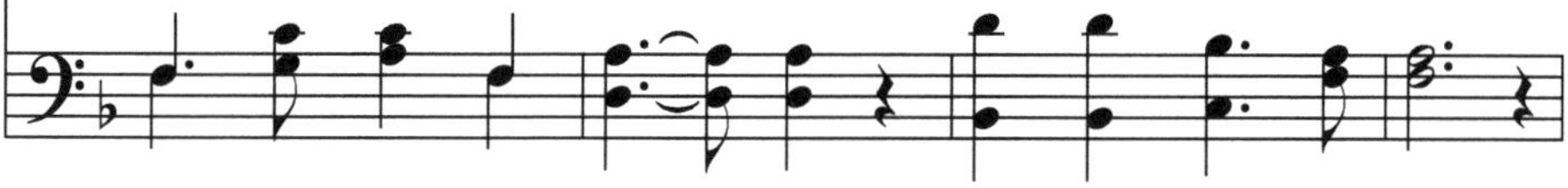

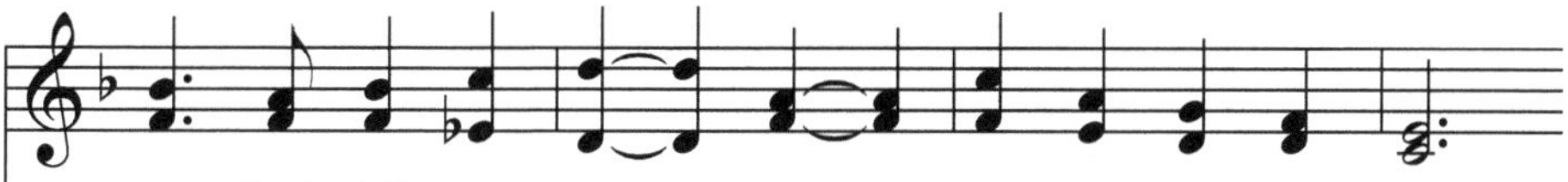

snow had fall - en, snow on snow, snow on snow,
in the bleak mid - win - ter a sta - ble place suf - ficed
but his moth - er on - ly, in her maid - en bliss,
if I were a wise man, I would do my part;

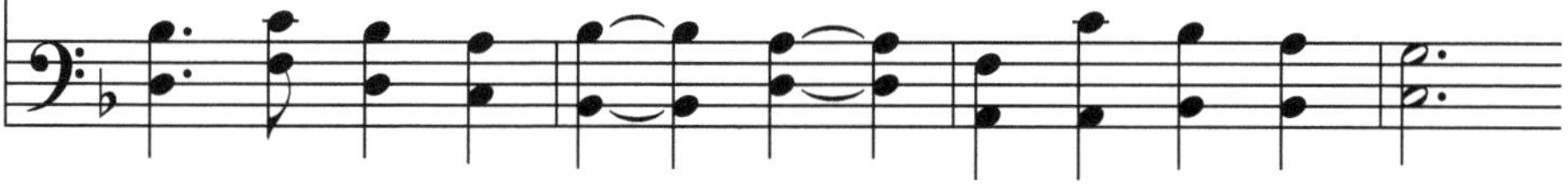

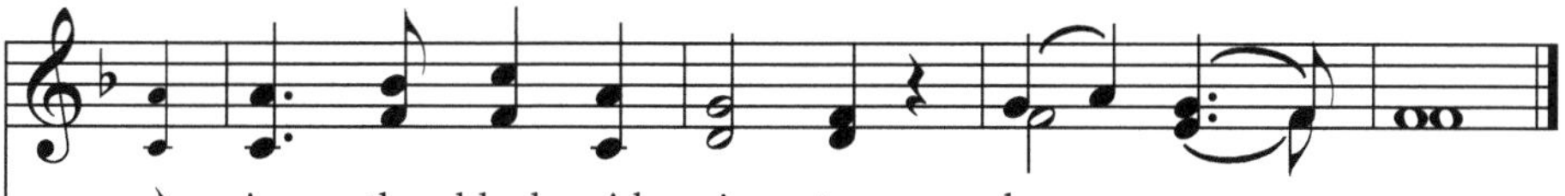

in the bleak mid - win - ter, long a - go.
the Lord God in - car - nate, Je - sus Christ.
wor - shiped the be - lov - ed with a kiss.
yet what I can I give him: give my heart.

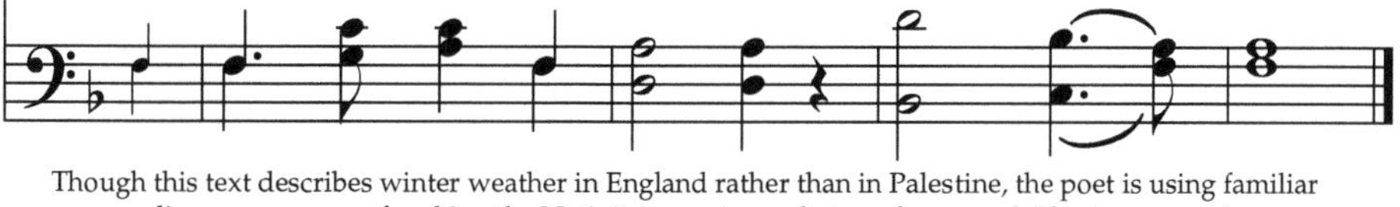

Though this text describes winter weather in England rather than in Palestine, the poet is using familiar surroundings as a means of making the Nativity more immediate and personal. The tune name honors a Gloucestershire village near the composer's birthplace in Cheltenham.

TEXT: Christina Rossetti, c. 1872, alt.
MUSIC: Gustav Holst, 1906

CRANHAM
Irregular

64
145
What Child Is This

1 What child is this, who, laid to rest, on Mary's lap is sleeping?
2 Why lies he in such mean estate where ox and ass are feeding?
3 So bring him incense, gold, and myrrh; come, one and all, to own him.

Whom angels greet with anthems sweet while shepherds watch are keeping?
Good Christian, fear; for sinners here the silent Word is pleading.
The King of kings salvation brings; let loving hearts enthrone him.

This, this is Christ the King, whom shepherds guard and angels sing;
Nails, spear, shall pierce him through; the cross be borne for me, for you.
Raise, raise the song on high. The virgin sings her lullaby.

haste, haste to bring him laud, the babe, the son of Mary!
Hail, hail, the Word made flesh, the babe, the son of Mary!
Joy, joy, for Christ is born, the babe, the son of Mary!

This Victorian text gains scope and power by having the original second halves of stanzas two and three restored. They give a stark forward glimpse of what lies ahead for this "babe, the son of Mary!" The tune is much older, dating from Tudor England.

TEXT: William Chatterton Dix, 1871
MUSIC: English ballad, 16th cent.; arr. *Christmas Carols New and Old,* 1871

GREENSLEEVES
8.7.8.7.6.8.6.7

65
146

Gentle Mary Laid Her Child

1 Gen-tle Mar-y laid her child low-ly in a man-ger;
2 An-gels sang a-bout his birth; wise men sought and found him;
3 Gen-tle Mar-y laid her child low-ly in a man-ger;

there he lay, the un-de-filed, to the world a strang-er.
heav-en's star shone bright-ly forth, glo-ry all a-round him.
he is still the un-de-filed, but no more a strang-er.

Such a babe in such a place, can he be the Sav-ior?
Shep-herds saw the won-drous sight, heard the an-gels sing-ing;
Son of God, of hum-ble birth, beau-ti-ful the sto-ry;

Ask the saved of all the race who have found his fa - vor.
all the plains were lit that night; all the hills were ring - ing.
praise his name in all the earth; hail the King of glo - ry!

This 20th-century Christmas text by an English-born Canadian clergyman was originally a poem called "The Manger Prince." It gains a certain antique flavor by being set to a late medieval song associated with springtime. (The tune name means "The flowering time is near.")

TEXT: Joseph Simpson Cook, 1919; rev. 1930
MUSIC: *Piae Cantiones,* 1582; arr. Ernest C. MacMillan, 1930

TEMPUS ADEST FLORIDUM
7.6.7.6.D

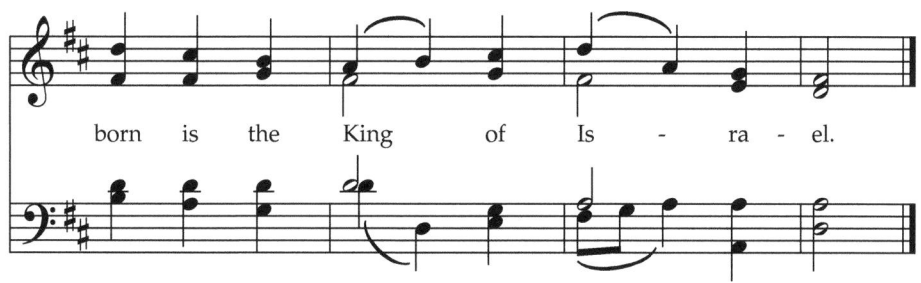

born is the King of Is - ra - el.

5 Then entered in those wise men three,
full reverently upon their knee,
and offered there in his presence
their gold, and myrrh, and frankincense.
Refrain

6 Then let us all with one accord
sing praises to our heavenly Lord,
that hath made heaven and earth of nought,
and with his blood our life hath bought.
Refrain

67
Mary and Joseph Came to the Temple 148

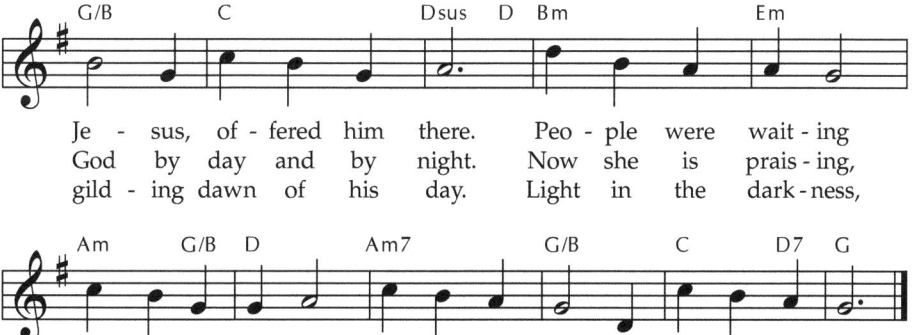

1 Mar-y and Jo-seph came to the tem-ple brought the boy
2 An-na had prayed there, wid-owed, long wait-ing, wor-ship-ing
3 Sim-e-on sings now: God prof-fers bless-ing, bril-liant-ly

Je - sus, of-fered him there. Peo - ple were wait - ing
God by day and by night. Now she is prais - ing,
gild - ing dawn of his day. Light in the dark - ness,

want - ing to greet him; long had they sought him, so - lace for care.
filled with e - la - tion: here is God's prom - ise, Christ is her light.
nev - er ex - tin-guished, Light of all na - tions, light up our way.

This text retells the story in Luke 2:22–39, usually called the Presentation of Christ in the Temple, which took place forty days after his birth. Mary, Joseph, and the Christ-child encounter there two devout people, Anna and Simeon, who identify this baby as the promised Messiah.

TEXT: Andrew Pratt, 1994
MUSIC: David Haas, 1985
Text © 1997 Stainer & Bell, Ltd. (admin. Hope Publishing Company)
Music © 1985 GIA Publications, Inc.

EVENING HYMN
5.5.5.4.D

As with Gladness Men of Old

69
150

1. As with gladness men of old did the guiding star behold;
as with joy they hailed its light, leading onward, beaming bright;
so, most gracious Lord, may we evermore be led to thee.

2. As with joyful steps they sped, Savior, to thy lowly bed,
there to bend the knee before thee, whom heaven and earth adore;
so may we with willing feet ever seek thy mercy seat.

3. As they offered gifts most rare at thy manger, rude and bare,
so may we with holy joy, pure and free from sin's alloy,
all our costliest treasures bring, Christ, to thee, our heavenly king.

4. Holy Jesus, every day keep us in the narrow way;
and when earthly things are past, bring our ransomed souls at last
where they need no star to guide, where no clouds thy glory hide.

The first three stanzas here use an as/so structure to draw parallels between the coming of the Magi and the spiritual lives of the singers, summed up in the prayer of the fourth stanza. Even though this adapted German tune was named for him, the author did not care for it.

TEXT: William Chatterton Dix, c. 1858
MUSIC: Conrad Kocher, 1838; abr. William Henry Monk, 1861; harm. *The English Hymnal*, 1906

DIX
7.7.7.7.7.7

70
151 We Three Kings of Orient Are

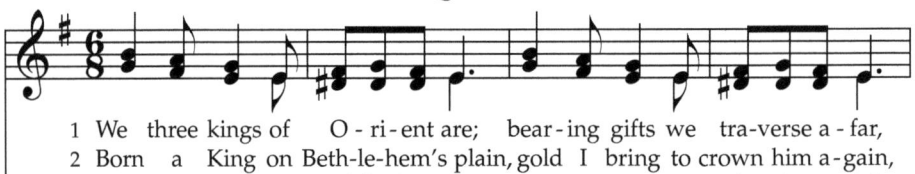

1 We three kings of O-ri-ent are; bear-ing gifts we tra-verse a-far,
2 Born a King on Beth-le-hem's plain, gold I bring to crown him a-gain,
3 Frank-in-cense to of-fer have I; in-cense owns a de-i-ty nigh;
4 Myrrh is mine; its bit-ter per-fume breathes a life of gath-er-ing gloom;
5 Glo-rious now be-hold him a-rise, King and God and Sac-ri-fice:

field and foun-tain, moor and moun-tain, fol-low-ing yon-der star.
King for-ev-er, ceas-ing nev-er o-ver us all to reign.
prayer and prais-ing glad-ly rais-ing, wor-ship-ing God Most High.
sor-rowing, sigh-ing, bleed-ing, dy-ing, sealed in the stone-cold tomb.
Al-le-lu-ia! Al-le-lu-ia! sounds through the earth and skies.

Refrain

O star of won-der, star of night, star with roy-al beau-ty bright,

west-ward lead-ing, still pro-ceed-ing, guide us to thy per-fect light!

Although Christians had begun by the 2nd century to speak of these visitors from eastern countries (Matthew 2:1–12) as "kings," perhaps because of passages like Psalm 72:10 and Isaiah 60:3, it is more accurate to think of them as magi or astrologers, the scholars of their day.

TEXT and MUSIC: John Henry Hopkins Jr., 1857, alt.

KINGS OF ORIENT
8.8.8.6 with refrain

What Star Is This, with Beams So Bright 71 / 152

1. What star is this, with beams so bright, more lovely than the noonday light? 'Tis sent to announce a newborn king, glad tidings of our God to bring.
2. 'Tis now fulfilled what God decreed, "From Jacob shall a star proceed"; and lo! the eastern sages stand to read in heaven the Lord's command.
3. While outward signs the star displays, an inward light the Lord conveys and urges them, with tender might, to seek the giver of the light.
4. O Jesus, while the star of grace impels us on to seek your face, let not our slothful hearts refuse the guidance of your light to use.

This 18th-century Latin text calls attention to three kinds of light: the light of the star leading the Magi to the Christ-child, the inward light inspiring their journey, and Christ who is the Light of the world. The simple unison melody unites everything in a gentle arc.

TEXT: Charles Coffin, 1736; trans. John Chandler, 1837, alt.
MUSIC: Trier ms., 15th cent.; adapt. Michael Praetorius, 1609; harm. George Ratcliffe Woodward, 1910

PUER NOBIS NASCITUR
LM
(alternate harmonization, 254)

Jesus Entered Egypt

73 / 154

Capo 5: (Am) (G) (Am) (C) (Am) (Dm) (Am)
Dm   C   Dm   F   Dm   Gm   Dm

1 Je - sus en - tered E - gypt flee-ing Her - od's hand,
2 Je - sus was a mi - grant liv - ing as a guest
3 Je - sus cross - es bor - ders with the wan - dering poor,

(C)   (G)   (Am)   (C) (Dm)
F   C   Dm   F   Gm

liv - ing as an a - lien in a for - eign land.
with the friends and strang - ers who could of - fer rest.
search-ing for a ref - uge, for an o - pen door.

(G)   (Em) (Am) (G)   (D) (G)
C   Am   Dm   C   G   C

Far from home and coun - try with his fam - i - ly,
Do we hold wealth light - ly so that we can share
Do our words and ac - tions an - swer Je - sus' plea:

(Am)   (G)   (Em) (Dm) (C) (G) (Am)
Dm   C   Am   Gm   F   C   Dm

was there room and wel - come for this ref - u - gee?
shel - ter with the home - less, and a - bun - dant care?
"Give the low - ly wel - come, and you wel - come me"?

Guitar chords do not correspond with keyboard harmony.

Human beings create divisions for many political, social, economic, and military reasons, but God is no respecter of the boundaries we erect. Jesus taught us to look for and respect the image of God that can be found in every human being, and to care for "the least of these."

TEXT: Adam M. L. Tice, 2007
MUSIC: Ralph Vaughan Williams, 1925
Text © 2009 GIA Publications, Inc.
Music © 1925 Oxford University Press

KING'S WESTON
6.5.6.5.D

74
155
Raise a Song of Gladness
Jubilate Deo

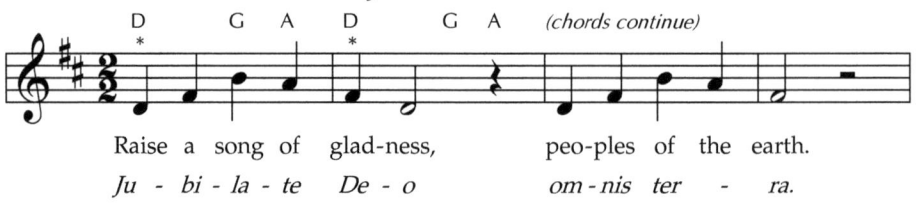

Raise a song of glad-ness, peo-ples of the earth.
Ju - bi - la - te De - o om - nis ter - ra.

Christ has come, bring-ing peace, joy to ev - ery heart.
Ser - vi - te Do - mi - no in lae - ti - ti - a.

Al - le - lu - ia, al - le - lu - ia, joy to ev - ery heart!
Al - le - lu - ia, al - le - lu - ia, in lae - ti - ti - a!

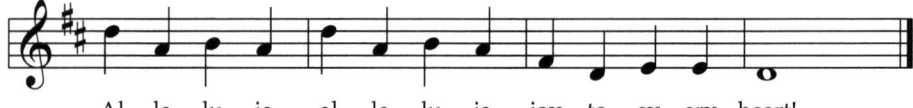

Al - le - lu - ia, al - le - lu - ia, joy to ev - ery heart!
Al - le - lu - ia, al - le - lu - ia, in lae - ti - ti - a!

*May be sung as a canon.

The Latin text here, for which the musical setting was originally composed, is from Psalm 100:1. The English paraphrase gives this verse a Christian interpretation, much as Isaac Watts did when he paraphrased Psalm 98 to produce "Joy to the World! The Lord Is Come" (see no. 53 [134]).

TEXT: Taizé Community, 1978
MUSIC: Jacques Berthier, 1978
Text and Music © 1979 Les Presses de Taizé (admin. GIA Publications, Inc.)

JUBILATE DEO
Irregular

COPYRIGHT HOLDER ACKNOWLEDGMENTS

A complete list of contact information for all copyright holders may be found online at www.pcusastore.com/hymnal.

- 3 (84)   *Text Alt.* © 1940 Church Pension Fund. Used by permission.
- 4 (85)   *Text and Music Arr.* © 1984 Fortress Press. All rights reserved. Used by permission of Augsburg Fortress.
- 5 (86)   *Text and Music* © 2009 GIA Publications, Inc. All rights reserved. Used by permission.
- 7 (88)   *Music Arr.* © 1990 John Weaver. All rights reserved. Used by permission.
- 8 (89)   *Text and Music* © 1982 GIA Publications, Inc. All rights reserved. Used by permission.
- 9 (90)   *Text and Music* © 1991 Les Presses de Taizé (admin. GIA Publications, Inc.). Used by permission. Responsive Reading of Psalm 27 from *An Inclusive-Language Psalter of the Christian People* © 1993 by Order of Saint Benedict. Published by Liturgical Press, Collegeville, Minnesota. Used with permission.
- 10 (91) *Text and Music* © 1995 GIA Publications, Inc. All rights reserved. Used by permission.
- 11 (92) *Text and Music* © 1986 Word Music, LLC (admin. WB Music Corp.). All rights reserved. Used by permission.
- 13 (94) *Text* © 2006 GIA Publications, Inc. All rights reserved. Used by permission. *Music Harm.* © 1978 *Lutheran Book of Worship*. Used by permission of Augsburg Fortress.
- 14 (95) *Text and Music* © 1984 Les Presses de Taizé (admin. GIA Publications, Inc.). All rights reserved. Used by permission.
- 17 (98) *Text and Music* © 1984 Hope Publishing Company, Carol Stream, IL 60188. All rights reserved. Used by permission.
- 18 (99) *Text* © 1978, 1987 Medical Mission Sisters. Used by permission. *Music* © 1943, 1961, 1985 Church Pension Fund. Used by permission.
- 19 (100) *Text and Music Arr.* © 1990 GIA Publications, Inc. All rights reserved. Used by permission.

20 (101)	*Text and Music* © 1992 WGRG, Iona Community (admin. GIA Publications, Inc.). All rights reserved. Used by permission.
21 (102)	*English Trans. Sts. 2–4* © 2006 Augsburg Fortress. All rights reserved. Used by permission.
22 (103)	*Text and Music* © 1988 Geonyong Lee. Used by permission.
24 (105)	*Text* © 1960 David Higham Associates, Ltd. All rights reserved. Used by permission. CAROL OF THE ADVENT (BESANÇON) music arranged by Martin Shaw (1875–1958) from *The Oxford Book of Carols* © Oxford University Press 1928. Reproduced by permission. All rights reserved.
25 (106)	*Text Adapt.* © 1982 Hope Publishing Company, Carol Stream, IL 60188. All rights reserved. Used by permission.
26 (107)	*Text and Music* © 1983 GIA Publications, Inc. All rights reserved. Used by permission.
28 (109)	*Text* © 1973 The Jubilate Group (admin. Hope Publishing Company). *Music* © 1983 Hope Publishing Company, Carol Stream, IL 60188. All rights reserved. Used by permission.
29 (110)	*Text* © 1996 LNWhymns.com (admin. Music Services). All rights reserved. ASCAP. *Music Arr.* © 2012 Eric T. Myers. Used by permission.
30 (111)	*Text* © 1978 *Lutheran Book of Worship*. Reprinted by permission of Augsburg Fortress.
32 (113)	*Music* © 1937, ren. 1965. H. Augustine Smith Jr., from the *New Church Hymnal*, Revell, a div. of Baker Publishing Group. All rights reserved. Used by permission.
39 (120)	*Text* © 1986 Concordia Publishing House. Used by permission. www.cph.org. *Music* © 1986 GIA Publications, Inc. All rights reserved. Used by permission.
41 (122)	*Korean Trans.* © The Christian Literature Society of Korea. Used by permission.
43 (124)	*Text and Music* © 1963, 1980 Walter Ehret and George K. Evans from *The International Book of Christmas Carols*. Used by permission of Walton Music Corporation.
44 (125)	*Text* © 1981 Concordia Publishing House. Used by permission. www.cph.org. *Music* © 1979 GIA Publications, Inc. All rights reserved. Used by permission.
45 (126)	*Music Harm.* © 1992 The Pilgrim Press. All rights reserved.

Used by permission. *Music Arr.* © 2000 Horace Clarence Boyer. Used by permission.

46 (127) *Music Arr.* © 2000 GIA Publications, Inc. All rights reserved. Used by permission.

50 (131) *Text* © 1990, 2000 Christian Conference of Asia (admin. GIA Publications, Inc.). All rights reserved. Used by permission. *Music* © 2010 Faith Alive Christian Resources. All rights reserved. Used by permission.

51 (132) *Music Harm.* © 1955, ren. 1983 John Ribble adapted from *The Hymnbook*. Used by permission of Westminster John Knox Press.

55 (136) *Music Harm.* © 1989 Melva Wilson Costen. All rights reserved. Used by permission.

56 (137) *Music Arr.* © 1986 WGRG, Iona Community (admin. GIA Publications, Inc.). All rights reserved. Used by permission.

57 (138) *Text and Music* © 1987, 2005 WGRG, Iona Community (admin. GIA Publications, Inc.). All rights reserved. Used by permission.

58 (139) *Text and Music* © 1969 Hope Publishing Company, Carol Stream, IL 60188. All rights reserved. Used by permission.

60 (141) *Christmas Song* ("On This Day Earth Shall Ring" [PERSONENT HODIE]. Latin words and melody from Piae Cantiones, 16th century. Melody arranged by Gustav Holst (1874–1934) for chorus and orchestra. English translation by Jane Marian Joseph (1894–1929). © 1924 J. Curwen & Sons Limited for the USA, France, Italy, Spain, Columbia, and Mexico. All rights reserved.

61 (142) *Music Arr.* © 1971 H. Barrie Cabena. Used by permission.

67 (148) *Text* © 1997 Stainer & Bell, Ltd. (admin. Hope Publishing Company, Carol Stream, IL 60188). All rights reserved. Used by permission. *Music* © 1985 GIA Publications, Inc. All rights reserved. Used by permission.

68 (149) *Music* © 1941 United Church Press. All rights reserved. Used by permission of The Pilgrim Press.

72 (153) "In Bethlehem a Newborn Boy" by Rosamond Herklots (1905–87). Reproduced by permission of Oxford University Press. All rights reserved. *Music* © 1983 Wilbur Held. All rights reserved.

73 (154)   *Text* © 2009 GIA Publications, Inc. All rights reserved. Used by permission. KING'S WESTON by Ralph Vaughn Williams (1872–1958) from *Enlarged Songs of Praise* by permission of Oxford University Press. All rights reserved.

74 (155)   *Text and Music* © 1979 Les Presses de Taizé (admin. GIA Publications, Inc.). All rights reserved. Used by permission.

75 (156)   *Text* © 1990 Hope Publishing Company, Carol Stream, IL 60188. All rights reserved. Used by permission.

Printed by Libri Plureos GmbH in Hamburg, Germany